MW00779198

FACE-TO-FACE WITH

ELIZABETH AND MARY

GENERATION *to* GENERATION

Five Sessions for
Individuals, M&M'S (Mentors & Mentees, Friends, Family) or Groups

with

Leader's Guide for Group-Study Facilitators,
and Session Guide

JANET THOMPSON

NEW HOPE
PUBLISHERS
Birmingham, Alabama

New Hope® Publishers
P. O. Box 12065
Birmingham, AL 35202-2065
www.newhopepublishers.com

New Hope Publishers is a division of WMU®.

Library of Congress Cataloging-in-Publication Data

Thompson, Janet.

Face-to-face with Elizabeth and Mary : generation to generation / Janet Thompson.

p. cm. -- (Face-to-face Bible study series)

"Five sessions for individuals, M&M'S (mentors & mentees, friends, family) or
groups with leader's guide for group-study facilitators, and session guide."

Includes bibliographical references and index.

ISBN-13: 978-1-59669-252-7 (sc : alk. paper)

ISBN-10: 1-59669-252-9 (sc : alk. paper) 1. Christian women--Religious life--
Textbooks. 2. Mentoring--Religious aspects--Christianity--Textbooks. 3. Elizabeth
(Mother of John the Baptist), Saint--Textbooks. 4. Mary, Blessed Virgin, Saint--
Textbooks. I. Title.

BV4529.18.T47 2010

259.082--dc22

2009035174

ISBN-10: 1-59669-252-9
ISBN-13: 978-1-59669-252-7

N094146 • 0210 • 4M1

DEDICATED WITH LOVE

To

Aunt Mae, a spiritual mother

Mentor spiritual mothers

My children—I pray I am a spiritual mother
as well as Mom

My grandchildren—as Grammie shares Jesus with you,
the next generation

TABLE OF CONTENTS

WELCOME

I began taking steps to start the Woman to Woman Mentoring Ministry while at my home church, Saddleback Church, in Lake Forest, California, pastored by Rick Warren. "Feed My sheep" was God's call and challenge to me to go into full-time ministry. God quickly revealed that *feeding* was mentoring and *the sheep* were women in churches all over the world. In obedience to the call, I launched the ministry in my home in January 1996, and we quickly outgrew my living room. After receiving numerous requests from other churches wanting to know how to start this type of a ministry, I authored *Woman to Woman Mentoring, How to Start, Grow, and Maintain A Mentoring Ministry DVD Leader Kit* (LifeWay Press).

As I traveled throughout the United States and Canada, training and speaking on mentoring, I heard numerous requests for a Bible study depicting God's plan for mentors and mentees— "M&M'S," as we fondly call them. One morning as my husband completed his quiet time with the Lord, Dave asked me if I had ever considered writing Bible studies based on mentoring relationships in the Bible. He knew that many M&M'S enjoy doing a Bible study together, and Dave felt that one focused on what God says about mentoring relationships would help answer many of the M&M'S questions.

After much prayer—and my husband's prodding—I decided to look in the Bible to see how many mentoring relationships I could find. Before long, I had discovered 12. This was my confirmation to begin writing the "Face-to-Face" Bible study series (formerly known as *Mentoring God's Way*). My passion and life mission is to help one generation of believers connect to the next generation and pass down God's plan for the Christian life. I trust that the "Face-to-Face" Bible study series will help you do exactly that.

WHAT IS MENTORING?

I love Dee Brestin's depiction of the informality of mentoring in *The Friendships of Women Workbook*: "It's not to be a dependent relationship, but simply a friendship as you spend time with a woman who is further down the road, at least in some areas of her Christian life. Win Couchman says, 'Mentoring works very nicely over a cup of coffee.'"

For those who like more concrete and specific definitions, *Roget's Super Thesaurus* provides this explanation of the root word of *mentoring*. It defines *mentor* as a teacher, guide, coach, or advisor. Most dictionaries define the word *mentor* as a trusted and wise counselor. To combine Dee's and the reference definitions with the Christian perspective: a Christian mentor is a spiritually mature woman who is a trusted and wise teacher, guide, coach, counselor, advisor, and friend. Thus, a *mentee* is someone willing to be taught, guided, coached, advised, or counseled by a trusted, wise, and spiritually older woman friend. Christian mentoring is sharing with another woman the many wonders you have seen God do in your life, and assuring her that He will do them in her life, too, as you both discover God's purpose and plan for your lives together.

Mentoring is not a hierarchy: it's always a two-way, mutually benefiting relationship where both participants learn from the other. Chris Tiegreen, author of my favorite devotional, *The One-Year Walk with God Devotional,* reminds us why it is always better to seek God's ways together:

> The Bible gives us solid wisdom on which to base our lives. But while it is absolute, its interpretation can vary widely. That's where advice comes in. Never underestimate the body of Christ. He has crafted us to live in community. Wisdom usually comes not to godly individuals but to godly fellowships. Are you seeking direction? Know your heart, but do not trust it entirely. Measure it by biblical wisdom and the counsel of those who follow it well.
> —June 27 devotional

The Bible also clearly instructs men to mentor men and women to mentor women. Titus 2:1–8 is the traditional "mentoring" passage:

> *You must teach what is in accord with sound doctrine. Teach the older men to be temperate, worthy of respect, self-controlled, and sound in faith, in love and in endurance. Likewise, teach the older*

women to be reverent in the way they live, not to be slanderers or addicted to much wine, but to teach what is good. Then they can train the younger women to love their husbands and children, to be self-controlled and pure, to be busy at home, to be kind, and to be subject to their husbands, so that no one will malign the word of God. Similarly, encourage the young men to be self-controlled. In everything set them an example by doing what is good. In your teaching show integrity, seriousness and soundness of speech that cannot be condemned, so that those who oppose you may be ashamed because they have nothing bad to say about us.

1 Peter 5:2–4 (NLT) could be addressing mentors:

Care for the flock that God has entrusted to you. Watch over it willingly, not grudgingly — not for what you will get out of it, but because you are eager to serve God. Don't lord it over the people assigned to your care, but lead them by your own good example. And when the Great Shepherd appears, you will receive a crown of never-ending glory and honor.

A mentor doesn't need to be an expert on the Bible or God, and she doesn't need to have a perfect life. If that were the case, none of us would qualify. A mentor simply needs to be willing to share her life experiences with another woman and be an example and role model of how a Christian woman does life. And how do we learn to be a godly role model? Answer: *"Remember your leaders who taught you the word of God. Think of all the good that has come from their lives, and follow the example of their faith"* (Hebrews 13:7 NLT).

Mentoring is not *doing* a ministry: It is *being* a godly woman who follows the Lord's command: *"One generation will commend your works to another; they will tell of your mighty acts"* (Psalm 145:4).

WHO ARE M&M'S?

In the Woman to Woman Mentoring Ministry, we lovingly refer to mentors and mentees as "M&M'S"—no, that's not the candy, although we always have M&M's® candy at our events. And just like the candy, there are varieties of M&M relationships—no two are the same. M&M'S may be—friends, acquaintances, family members, workers, neighbors, members of a mentoring or other ministry, team members, women with similar life experiences, or any two women—who want to grow spiritually together.

M&M'S AND MORE!

The "Face-to-Face" Bible study series has a variety of applications. You can enjoy this study:
* On your own
* As a mentor and mentee (M&M'S) in a mentoring or discipleship relationship
* Between two friends
* Between two relatives
* As a small or large group studying together
* As a churchwide Bible study

The Bible studies offer three types of questions:
* ON YOUR OWN: questions for doing the study individually
* M&M'S: questions for mentors and mentees, two friends, or relatives studying together
* ON YOUR OWN AND M&M'S: questions applicable to both individuals and those studying together
* GROUPS: answer all the questions, with a Leader's/Facilitator's Guide in each book

STUDY FORMAT

There are five main sessions, comprised of five study days. Each day's study includes:
* Scriptures and questions for you to study and answer
* Face-to-Face Reflections—a discussion of the day's topic

- Personal Parable—a story depicting and applying the day's topic
- Mentoring Moment—take-away wisdom for the day

At the end of each session there is:
- Faith in Action—an opportunity for life application of the lessons learned
- Let's Pray Together—a prayer for me to pray with you

Following session five are Closing Materials:
♦ Let's Pray a Closing Prayer Together
♦ Janet's Suggestions—ideas for further study
♦ Leader's Guide for Group-Study Facilitators and M&M'S
♦ Session Guide
♦ Prayer & Praise Journal

SUGGESTIONS FOR INDIVIDUAL STUDY

I admire you for seeking out this study on your own and having the desire and discipline to work on it by yourself. I like to grow in the knowledge of the Lord and His Word and have found that my most relevant insights from God come when I seek Him by myself in a quiet place. Have fun on your own, and share with someone all you are learning.

1. A good way to stay consistent in your studying is to work a little each day during your quiet time in the morning or evening.

2. Tell someone you have started this study, and ask him or her to keep you accountable to complete it.

SUGGESTIONS FOR M&M'S— MENTORS AND MENTEES, FRIENDS, AND RELATIVES

I hope the study of *Face-to-Face with Elizabeth and Mary: Generation to Generation* adds a new dimension to your M&M relationship. Here are a few study tips.

1. Come to your meetings prepared to discuss your answers to the session's questions.

2. Or you may decide to answer the questions together during your meetings.

3. If you don't live near each other, you can have phone or online discussions.

4. Remember, the questions are to enlighten and not divide; be honest and open, but also loving and kind.

SUGGESTIONS FOR GROUP STUDY

I love group studies because you get to hear other people's points of view and lasting friendships often develop. Your meetings should be fun, informative, relevant, and applicable to group members' lives. Enjoy yourself with your fellow sisters in Christ, but remember that joining a group study *does* mean commitment. So please attend your scheduled meetings, unless there is a real emergency. I suggest the following courtesies:

1. Put the meeting dates on your calendar.

2. Commit to doing your study and come prepared to discuss it. This honors the rest of the group, and you will get so much more from the sessions.

3. Ask questions—because, chances are, someone else has the same question.

4. Participate in the discussion, but be cautious of dominating the conversation. For example, if you have answered several questions, even though you know all the answers, let someone else have a turn. Try to encourage a less outgoing member to share.

5. Listen when others speak and give each speaker your full attention.

6. Arrive on time.

7. Keep in confidence the information shared in the group.

LEADERS AND FACILITATORS

When I lead and facilitate Bible-study groups, I value a complete and detailed Leader's Guide, so that is what I have provided for you. The "Face-to-Face" Bible study series has a Leader's Guide at the end of each book to provide the leader/facilitator with creative ideas for:

1. Guiding group discussion

2. Adding life application and variety to the sessions

3. Accommodating the varied learning styles of the group (visual learners, hands-on learners, auditory learners, and more)

TO YOU–THE READER

Whatever way you are doing this study, God has a message and a lesson just for you. Here are some suggestions I pray will enhance your experience studying *Face-to-Face with Elizabeth and Mary*.

1. Start each session with prayer and ask the Lord to speak to you through the Scripture readings, the prayerful answering of the questions, and the interaction with others.

2. Set your own pace. I provide breaking points, but make it comfortable for yourself and break as you need to do so.

3. If you're not sure how to answer a question, move on; but continue praying and thinking about the answer. Often my answers come quickly, but God's answers are the most fruitful.

4. Unless otherwise indicated, all the questions relate to NIV Bible passages. Lists of Scriptures are sequential, as they appear in

the Bible. You will be looking up Scripture references in your Bible, which is an invaluable way to study and learn about the Bible.

5. Use the space provided to answer questions, but don't feel obligated to fill the space. However, if you need more room, continue answering in a separate journal.

6. A book effectively used for study should be underlined, highlighted, and comments written in the margins, so interact with the material.

7. At the end of session five, you will find suggestions from me on books to read or activities to delve deeper into what God may be teaching you about the biblical M&M relationship featured in the study.

8. Use the Prayer & Praise Journal starting on page 139 to record the mighty work God does in your life during this study. Journal prayer requests and note when God answers.

9. Have some chocolate. After reading about M&M'S throughout the study, you'll be ready for some candy!

My heart, admiration, and encouragement go out to you with this book. I pray that mentoring becomes a vital part of your life. The "Face-to-Face" Bible study series is another way the Lord allows me to "feed My sheep." And I hope that you will enjoy this and other "Face-to-Face" Bible studies and "feed" others as well.

About His Work,
Janet

SESSION ONE
FACE-TO-FACE WITH ELIZABETH AND MARY:
GENERATION *to* GENERATION

THEIR STORY

Can You Relate?

*D*uring a mother-daughter chat with my daughter Michelle, I mentioned my desire to tell her sister, Kim, a vital truth relevant to Kim's spiritual growth as a new Christian. Michelle's response was wise, but hard for me to hear: "It's probably better that Kim hears this from someone else. You know that kids always listen more to advice from women other than their mom. We don't think Mom can be objective when it comes to us."

Oh, did these words sting! I knew this is true because I had a similar reaction to my mom's advice, and it made her so mad. I would come home with some great revelation my friend's mom had said, and my mom would admonish me: "I said the same thing to you!"

Often, we feel our moms are prejudiced and biased when it comes to us. Or we fear they have their own agenda and motives, so we seek out someone whom we feel will give us uncensored advice and answers to our questions.

Now I get it! My constant prayer is for my daughters to seek out a "spiritual mom" to advise them when I'm not physically near, or inexperienced in the area of concern, or too close to the situation to be objective. I pray the spiritual mom whom they choose will be a godly woman: someone wise and compassionate who will guide my daughters in the path of righteousness. Mary found such a spiritual mother in Elizabeth.

Day One

How Does Elizabeth and Mary's Story Relate to Us?

The story of Elizabeth and Mary is a beautiful example of a "spiritual mothering" mentoring relationship. Let's look at how their story might apply to our relationships today.

On Your Own and M&M's

Q: You may have read Luke 1:5–80 many times, but please stop now and read with an eye towards discovering God's purpose and plan in bringing Elizabeth and Mary together.

- What impresses you the most about this story?

- What, if anything, seems unusual to you?

- What new insights did God reveal?

Q: Do you see any similarities between Elizabeth and Mary's story and your own story?

FACE-TO-FACE REFLECTIONS

We see God's plan for Elizabeth and Mary to be together during this eventful time for them. Many times mentors and mentees, and/or friends and family, gravitate towards each other when something similar happens in their lives. Mentoring is nothing more than sharing with another woman those "been-there-done-that" experiences in life, where God helped you through, and He will help her too!

In the Woman to Woman Mentoring Ministry, we use intercessory prayer to match women into M&M relationships. M&M'S often find they have things in common that only God knew. Discovering these commonalities confirms to them that God truly was instrumental in bringing their lives together in a mentoring relationship, just as He intervened to bring Elizabeth and Mary together.

PERSONAL PARABLE

I personally know the joy of God intervening to bring me together with a young woman looking for a mentor. Kristen was 25 years younger than me, and still living at home with Mom and Dad, when she visited a young women's Bible study group that my daughter, Shannon, led in our home. Several weeks after receiving the "feed My sheep" call that I mentioned in the welcome on page 6, Shannon's group asked me to join them. I thought these young women, who were hungry to learn about the Lord, must be the "sheep" God wanted fed, so I gladly accepted their invitation to be the group mentor.

When Kristen introduced herself to the group, she said she was home for summer break from a Christian college and a summer assignment was to find a mentor. This was the first time Kristen and I had ever met, but she looked straight at me and asked *me* if I would be her mentor.

I sensed Kristen was another "sheep" God wanted me to "feed," so I agreed to mentor her over the summer. It was becoming clear to me that *feeding* meant *mentoring*. My experience mentoring Kristen helped me launch the Woman to Woman Mentoring Ministry at Saddleback Church.

Kristen was at a crossroads in her Christian life, trying to balance a boyfriend, school, ministry, work, friends, and family. She wanted to feel safe and secure in working through issues with a woman who would give her a godly perspective without having a personal stake in the outcome. I knew she didn't need me to be her mom. Kristen had a wonderful mom, but she was asking me to be her spiritual mom. We decided that my role in her life would be:

- a guide to and through the Scriptures
- a listening ear
- a prayer partner
- an accountability partner
- and most importantly, a role model of the Christian woman she wanted to become

* * *

Mentoring Moment

Susan Hunt says in her book *Spiritual Mothering*: "No matter how solid our relationships are with our biological daughters, their lives will be richer if they are also nurtured by other women ... our biological connection sometimes blurs our vision."

* * *

Day Two

What Is a Spiritual Mother?

The term *spiritual mothering* may be new to you, but it simply depicts the nurturing element of some mentoring relationships. Let's explore the appropriate use of the title and why Elizabeth so beautifully embodies the expression.

On Your Own and M&M's

The American Heritage Dictionary of the English Language defines *mother*: "a female that has borne an offspring. A female who has adopted a child or otherwise established a maternal relationship with another person." *Mothering* means "to give birth to...to create and care for; instigate and carry through. To watch over, nourish, and protect."

Q: Based on those definitions, write your own definition of *spiritual mother*.

Q: Review the mentoring discussion on pages 6–9. How does spiritual mothering embody mentoring?

- What are differences and similarities between the two terms?

- How does *spiritual mother* relate to *mentor*?

Q: Would you characterize your relationship as spiritual
   mothering? Why or why not?

FACE-TO-FACE REFLECTIONS

Not every young woman has a Christian or even loving mother.
Many young women find themselves spiritually alone, as the only
Christian in their family or circle of friends. Our mobile society
separates mothers and daughters by many miles, or they find
themselves dealing with things to which Mom can't always relate.

PERSONAL PARABLE

Kristen had a loving mom and dad, but it was difficult
for her to discuss with them her spiritual questions and
challenges. I had daughters Kristen's age, so when she
asked me to be her spiritual mentor, we both knew that I
also would be giving her a mother's perspective. However,
it was important for both of us to remember that I was not
Kristen's mom and she was not my daughter. Establishing
that boundary allowed me to remain more objective and
Kristen was receptive to my advice and suggestions.

Mentoring Moment

"My working definition for the spiritual mothering relationship is
this: When a woman possessing faith and spiritual maturity enters
into a nurturing relationship with a younger woman in order to
encourage and equip her to live for God's glory.... Please note
that giving birth biologically or being of a certain chronological
age are not prerequisites for spiritual mothers."
— Susan Hunt, *Spiritual Mothering*

DAY THREE

CHARACTERISTICS OF
A SPIRITUAL MOTHER

everal Bible translations state that Elizabeth and Zechariah were *"righteous in God's sight or God's eyes,"* and Matthew 1:19 (NIV) says that Mary's husband, Joseph, *"was a righteous man."* Let's explore the word *righteous*, a term used 512 times in the Bible.

ON YOUR OWN AND M&M'S

Q: Proverbs always is a good place to go for insight. From the following verses, list characteristics of a righteous person, and then write a definition of *righteous*.

- Proverbs 10:21
- Proverbs 10:31
- Proverbs 12:5
- Proverbs 13:6
- Proverbs 13:9
- Proverbs 21:21
- Proverbs 23:24
- Proverbs 29:7
- Proverbs 29:27

Q: Luke 1:5–6 tells us that *both* Jewish priest Zechariah and his wife, Elizabeth, were descendants of Aaron and the priestly division of Abijah. Read Exodus 4:14–16, Exodus 28:1–3, and 1 Chronicles 24:1,10. Why would this heritage be significant?

• What can you surmise about Elizabeth and Zechariah's spiritual life, as a couple?

• What kind of marriage do you think they had?

Q: Based on Luke 1:5–6 and your definition of *righteous*, what were Elizabeth's character qualities?

Q: What was one of Elizabeth's heartaches (Luke 1:7)?

• What did Elizabeth endure due to barrenness (Luke 1:25)?

• Knowing her character, how do you think she reacted to this?

Q: Read Proverbs 31:25–30 and Hebrews 13:7. What characteristics would you look for in a mentor/spiritual mother?

Q: After answering the above questions, why do you think Elizabeth made an excellent spiritual mother for young Mary?

M & M'S

Q: Mentee, what characteristics do you appreciate in your mentor? Note them here and tell her the next time you meet.

FACE-TO-FACE REFLECTIONS

Both Elizabeth and Zechariah were upright in God's sight. He was a priest serving at the temple. Elizabeth was of priestly descent; in Hebrew, her name means "my God is an oath." This elderly, devout Jewish couple observed *all* of the Lord's commandments and regulations *blamelessly* (Luke 1:6). Can anyone living today say he or she adheres to *all* the Lord's commandments? While imperfect, they were truly a righteous couple, wholly devoted to God.

However, the NIV Bible notes "the lack of children…was generally considered to indicate divine disfavor and often brought social reproach." And Zechariah, having no child to carry on his name, would have been within his rights to seek another wife. He didn't. Rather, the couple remained faithful to each other and faithful to God.

Though Jewish culture regarded childlessness as a reproach from God, this couple never blamed God or became bitter and resentful. Instead, they continued steadfastly worshipping and serving Him.

It's important when seeking out a mentor or spiritual mother to look at her life and relationships. Is she a godly woman inside and outside her home? If she is married, does she have a loving relationship with her husband, and is he a godly man? Do they study God's Word and pray together in their home, and how does she handle life's difficulties? Do you admire her and the way she lives her life? Would you characterize her as a "righteous woman"? Does she love Jesus?

PERSONAL PARABLE

Kristen asked me to mentor her because she recognized we had many things in common, and I had a life she admired and desired to achieve for herself. She wanted to go into ministry: I was in ministry. She wanted a Christian marriage and to be a godly wife and mother: I was living out those roles. She wanted to further her Christian education: I was in seminary. She saw I had some "been-there-done-that" experiences and could use what God had taught me in those situations to guide her through her own challenges.

Mentoring Moment

Wisdom is caught, not taught.

Day Four

Finding a Spiritual Mother

W e do not choose our earthly mothers—essentially, they choose us by being the vessel through which we receive life. Spiritual mothers may or may not choose us. Often we have to do the seeking and selecting.

On Your Own and M&M's

Q: Gabriel visited Mary *"in the sixth month"* (Luke 1:26). To what was this time frame referring?

Q: Why do you think God allowed elderly Elizabeth to conceive six months before the Holy Spirit *"came upon"* young Mary?

Q: What were the prophetic reasons?
- Isaiah 40:3–5
- Mark 1:1–8; Luke 1:13–17, 3:4–6

Q: Read Hebrews 13:7 again. Why did the angel Gabriel tell Mary about Elizabeth in Luke 1:34–37?

• What did Mary do as soon as the angel left her (Luke 1:39–40)?

Q: In what areas of your life would you like to find someone who made it through a "been–there-done-that" experience, who can provide hope and encouragement that, with God's help, you'll make it too?

Q: What are some experiences in your own life that God could use to help someone else?

Q: Where might you find a spiritual mother, or a young woman seeking a spiritual mother?

Q: God spoke through an angel to direct Mary to Elizabeth. What should you do first when seeking a spiritual mother, or desiring to be a spiritual mother?
• Matthew 21:22; Mark 11:24

ON YOUR OWN

Q: Consider why you need to seek out a spiritual mother, or where God could use you to be a spiritual mother.

M & M'S

Q: Why do you think God brought the two of you together?

FACE-TO-FACE REFLECTIONS

Just like Mary, Elizabeth was a woman chosen by God to carry out a divine mission. In Luke 1:36, Gabriel provides the historical landmark of Mary being blessed with a miracle child in the sixth month of Elizabeth's own miracle pregnancy. Scripture confirmed that Elizabeth's child, John the Baptist, would be the forerunner of Mary's child, Jesus Christ, the anticipated Messiah.

Gabriel also was setting the stage for a mentoring relationship: a shared-experience, role-modeling, spiritual-mothering relationship. Mary didn't waste any time after Gabriel's visit. Without even sending a message ahead to Elizabeth, Mary showed up at Elizabeth's door and received a warm greeting from her relative, who soon would become a mother and a mentoring spiritual mother.

PERSONAL PARABLE

When I met Kristen, I was just beginning to learn about mentoring. I only knew what I had read in books, but I was willing to share with Kristen whatever insight, wisdom, and experience I had gleaned.

Kristen was very bold and courageous showing up on my doorstep and asking me to mentor her. She set herself up for rejection if I had said no, but she determined it was worth the risk of me saying yes. And what a mighty work God did in and through our relationship, just as He did with Elizabeth and Mary, and He will do for you too.

* * *

Mentoring Moment

We have not because we ask not.

* * *

DAY FIVE

WOMEN OF FAITH

A central theme of Elizabeth and Mary's story is the women's unquestioning faith.

ON YOUR OWN AND M&M'S

Q: Read Genesis 18:1–15; Matthew 1:19–24; Luke 1:8–20, 26–38, 41–42; and 2:25–27. How did God speak to:
- Abraham
- Sarah
- Zechariah
- Joseph
- Elizabeth
- Mary
- Simeon

Q: Read Genesis 15:1–6. How does Abraham's response resemble Elizabeth's, Mary's, and Joseph's responses?

Q: Read Genesis 18:12. How does Sarah's response resemble that of Zechariah?

Q: Do you see any scriptural evidence in Luke 1:26–38 that this might have been Mary's first profession of faith?

Q: Had Mary not become a believer, or maybe even as a believer, list excuses she might have given Gabriel for not agreeing to God's plans for her.

Q: Read Isaiah 7:13–14. What prophecy (confirmed by Matthew 1:22–23) was fulfilled by Mary saying yes to God?

Q: How did Zechariah "happen" to be in the temple the day Gabriel spoke to him (Luke 1:8–9)?

• Was this chance or God's intervention? Why?

Q: Look up the following verses that help us begin "seeing" life from God's perspective.
• Psalm 25:15   • Psalm 123:2
• Psalm 101:3   • Psalm 141:8
• Psalm 119:18

Q: Read Luke 1:37 and Romans 8:28. What assurance do we have as faithful believers that God is in *every* aspect of our lives?

Q: Read John 20:29, Romans 8:24–25, and Hebrews 11:1. If you are a believer and haven't yet seen the unseen in your life, what does the Bible say about your faith?

Q: What do John 3:18 and Romans 8:1 say is the unbeliever's fate?

Q: Read Hebrews chapter 11, referred to as the "hall of faith." While the text doesn't mention Elizabeth and Mary, they were women of faith. Write a paragraph about their faith that would fit into this chapter.

Q: Describe a time in your life when you knew that God was

orchestrating a circumstance, but no one believed you, or shunned the idea that it was God rather than coincidence.

- Did their disbelief shake your faith?

- Did you try to convince them of God's involvement and use the opportunity to profess your faith, or ignore their disbelief?

Q: Describe another time when you acted in faith and were blessed.

Q: Write the number of times the letter *f* occurs here: "The father of the bride paid for half of the festivities; the unpaid balance of the bill he left for his new son-in-law as a wedding gift." Do you see five...six...seven? Look in Face-to-Face Reflections below for the correct answer.

M & M'S

Q: Mentor, if the mentee is struggling with unbelievers' reactions to her faith, discuss ways she might respond in love to doubters.

Q: Mentor, share examples with your mentee of seeing God work in miraculous "unseen" ways in your life and how it has strengthened your faith.

FACE-TO-FACE REFLECTIONS

Historians tell us that there were approximately 20,000 priests in Israel during Zechariah's ministry. A priest was selected to attend to the incense in the temple by casting lots: whoever picked the longest stick or arrow or won the throw of rocks. Some priests went their entire career without ever entering the inner temple. It surely was not chance that Zechariah won the cast of lots, and it probably was a once-in-a-lifetime opportunity. God intervened for Zechariah to enter the temple at this specific time in history because He had a heavenly messenger waiting for him inside.

Likewise, it wasn't chance that Mary went to see Elizabeth. God knew that Elizabeth was the perfect spiritual mother for Mary, because not everyone would have believed either of their miraculous stories of God's supernatural intervention. And Mary's visit confirmed God's plans for Zechariah and Elizabeth's, and Mary's unborn sons.

Even fellow believers often fail to acknowledge supernatural occurrences. They look for a rational element or consider something a coincidence instead of giving God the recognition and glory He deserves. This is one of the main arguments between science and Christianity. Science looks for a logical, scientifically provable reason behind every occurrence or phenomenon. In a promotional trailer for the controversial movie *Angels and Demons*, the actor Tom Hanks's character, Robert Langdon, a Harvard symbologist, has a telling mind-versus-heart discussion with a priest who asks him:

Priest: "Do you believe in God, sir?"

Langdon: "Father, I simply believe that religion... "

Priest interrupts: "I didn't ask if you believe what man says about God. I asked if *you* believe in God."

Langdon: "I'm an academic. My mind tells me I will never understand God."

Priest: "And your heart?"

Langdon: "Tells me I'm not meant to. Faith is a gift that I have yet to receive."

The foundation of the Christian life is the gift of faith that we freely receive by asking Jesus into our heart. Believers should look for the hand of God in *every* circumstance. Recognizing God's supernatural intervention and operations comes with spiritual maturity. The Bible says that believers who have yet to see God's involvement in their life, but still believe, will be rewarded for their patience and unquestioning faith. But in reality, becoming a Christian is evidence of a divine revelation in every believer's life.

It takes real courage and fortitude to stand strong when the world is trying to undermine your belief system. That's why it's so important for Christians to gather and worship together corporately at church and in small groups, and form mentoring relationships to:

encourage each other, pray together, study God's Word, and remind each other that Jesus is real and alive today in every believer's life. Nothing happens by chance to a believer.

The correct answer to the number of *f*'s in the riddle question is ten! I found this exercise in *Walk Thru the Bible's Daily Walk*, April 9, 2009. The accompanying commentary advised: "It's one thing to have 'eyes to see' hidden letters in a sentence, but infinitely more significant to have eyes to see God at work in the world around you."

PERSONAL PARABLE

God has blessed and humbled me with numerous Holy Spirit, supernatural interventions in my life. I am sure we all experience these faith-strengthening interventions daily, but sometimes they're easy to dismiss when we aren't looking for them. I try to look for the presence of God every waking moment, and I see the unseen abundantly in my life.

On page 6 of the welcome, I mentioned that "Feed My sheep" was God's call for me to go into full-time ministry. Let me share with you the details of that believable "unbelievable" story.

I attended a Women in Leadership conference in Portland, Oregon, with the express purpose of discovering what type of ministry was available to women who didn't want to work with women. The second night of the conference, as I was sipping coffee after dinner and waiting for the keynote speaker to take the stage, I suddenly heard the words "Feed My sheep." I looked around the table to see who was talking about sheep, but no one was talking to me. In my mind, I said: *What sheep where and what would I feed them if I found them?* I simply heard the words again, "Feed My sheep," to which I responded, "OK!" Later back in my room, I called my husband and we prayed for the Holy Spirit to reveal to me the meaning of those words, if indeed this command was from God.

The next morning, to my shock, the speaker based her talk on John 21:15–17 where Jesus is telling Peter, "If you love me, feed My sheep." The speaker's topic was "Shepherding Women in Your Church." God was asking me to do the very thing I didn't want to do, but I had said "Ok." The Woman to Woman Mentoring Ministry was the result of me faithfully responding to the continual promptings of the Holy Spirit. I've been listening for and responding to that still small voice ever since.

Mentoring Moment

"Faith is to believe what you do not see;
the reward of this faith is to see what you believe."
—St. Augustine

FAITH IN ACTION

What one thing from this session does God want you to apply in your life today?

LET'S PRAY TOGETHER

Lord, we want to be obedient to Your call on our life. The world often pulls us into its snares and we need the Holy Spirit helping us fight against that current. Even though we feel like a fish swimming up stream, we want to be used by You, Lord, and we want to be encouragers to our fellow believers. Help us find spiritually wise women to answer our questions and give us encouragement, and let us do the same for those spiritually younger women who You put in our life. Praise God that You are alive and so visible in our world today. Amen.

WE ARE FAMILY

Day One

How Will Spiritual Mothering Affect My Family?

*T*he Bible doesn't mention Mary's mother, so we don't know if she was still alive. But considering Mary was probably a teenager, it's likely her mom was living.

ON YOUR OWN AND M&M's

Q: How soon did Mary leave for Elizabeth's house after Gabriel's visit (Luke 1:38–39)?

Q: Why might Mary spend three months with her relative Elizabeth, instead of staying home with her mother (assuming her mom was still living), during this eventful time of her life?

Q: Were any of the reasons you mentioned the same reasons you might seek out a spiritual mother in your life? Yes? No?

- If yes, how do these reasons apply to your life today?

- If no, what are different reasons you might seek out a spiritual mother?

Q: How do you think Mary's mother reacted to Mary's trip?

Q: If your mother is still living, how would she react if you went to someone else for personal or spiritual mentoring?

Q: If you have a daughter, how would she feel about you mentoring another young woman?

M&M'S

Q: Discuss any concerns that family members have about your M&M relationship.

FACE-TO-FACE REFLECTIONS

There could have been a number of reasons Mary traveled alone to see Elizabeth. Maybe her mother didn't understand or believe what was happening to Mary. Mom's reaction could have been shock, judgment, or fear of what others would say—an unwed mother disgraced the entire family. Mom might have told Mary to leave town, perhaps even saying she was no longer welcome in her home.

Mom may have feared for Mary's safety; under Old Testament law an unwed mother faced possible punishment by stoning. Maybe she thought, *Will Joseph go through with the marriage, or might we have the unhappy chore of canceling the wedding?* There would have been so many questions and speculations—perhaps she thought it would be best if Mary were gone during all of this to spare her and the family humiliation.

Or a more loving and wiser response would have been for Mary's mom to encourage her daughter to visit their relative Elizabeth, whom they just learned was also experiencing a miraculous pregnancy. Mom could have been intuitive enough to know that she could not relate to Mary as well as someone who was in a similar circumstance. They also might have agreed that Mary could be a comfort and help to Elizabeth in her last months of pregnancy.

PERSONAL PARABLE

When Kristen asked me to mentor her, I needed to know her mom supported this. She talked with her mom about it, arranged our meeting, and we had Mom's blessing.

But we didn't have Kristen's boyfriend's blessing. He was uncomfortable because Kristen and I talked often about her desire to stay sexually pure, under great temptation.

Sensitive to my daughters' feelings about me extending attention and time to another young woman, I had them meet her, and tried to plan activities for us to do together. My time with Kristen didn't interfere with family plans and activities, and I didn't talk to them about Kristen's issues.

I caution mentors who are moms to talk with their daughters to assure them that the mentee is not replacing them. Moms need to be aware of their own daughters' possible jealousy or unwillingness to share her; this is a natural reaction, so don't chastise or over-look your daughters' behavior. Use their feelings as an opportunity to talk candidly about the value of men-toring and encourage them to find a spiritual mother. Explain *spiritual mothering* and the reasons you're extending yourself to another young woman. It might be beneficial to invite the mentee to some family functions so the girls can meet, and hopefully, have a friendly relationship.

If friction in your home over being a mentor or spiritual mother to a young woman remains, it might be best to wait until your daughters are out of the house. For now, choose to mentor a woman older than your daughters' ages.

● ● ●

Mentoring Moment

We should raise our daughters, and spiritual daughters, to be progres-sively independent of us and completely dependent on the Lord.

● ● ●

Day Two

Mentoring Our Family

*S*ome Bible translations say Elizabeth is a kinswoman of Mary. In Luke 1:36, the NIV Bible calls her a *"relative."* Many scholars feel she could have been a cousin, possibly an aunt, or even just of the same tribe. What we know for sure is that Elizabeth and Mary were related.

On Your Own and M&M's

Q: Read 1 Timothy 5:8. How does this speak to you about being available for other family members?

Q: Usually there's a favorite aunt, grandma, sister, other relative, or close family friend who always seems to understand you when no one else does. Who has been that "family mentor" for you?

• How does talking with this person help you?

• How does your asking questions or confiding in this person encourage him or her?

- Had you thought before about your relative benefiting from your relationship?

Q: Do you think God might be calling you to mentor someone in your family?

- What steps could you take to make that happen?

M & M'S

Q: If either of you have had a family member be an Elizabeth to you, or you have been an Elizabeth to a family member, share those stories with each other.

FACE-TO-FACE REFLECTIONS

We live hurried and busy lives, and many families live a great distance from each other. Consequently, families often don't take time for each other unless there is a crisis. Technology makes it possible to stay connected, but there is nothing like sitting down together for a cup of coffee or tea and a chat.

Church mentoring ministries are a passion of mine because so many women don't have family living near them, and as we'll discuss tomorrow, believers are all in the family of God.

PERSONAL PARABLE

I hope that I am a spiritual role model for my children, and they know that I am available whenever they need me, both spiritually and personally. Currently, only one of our three daughters, Shannon, lives near us, and we get together regularly as a family to visit and catch up on each other's lives. Shannon often asks me questions or confides in me about personal issues, and I cherish those conversations.

Daughter Kim lives miles away in another state, so we have a family plan on our cell phones and we talk and email regularly. While it's not the same as being together, I work hard at being a relevant and integral part of her life. Yet another daughter, Michelle, lived out of the country for eight years, and we weren't able to be as involved in each other's lives, but it always blessed me when she emailed her dad and me for prayer requests.

Michelle's family has since moved back to the States, but not our state. So we now have the family plan cell phone program with her too, as well as with our son, Sean, and daughter-in-law, Janel, who live in yet another state! In my book *Face-to-Face with Naomi and Ruth*, I discuss my desire to be a Naomi "spiritual mother-in-law" in Janel's life.

Mentoring Moment

In her book *Spiritual Mothering*, Susan Hunt said about relatives, Elizabeth and Mary: "What happened between these two women is the essence of spiritual mothering. When women do for other women what Elizabeth did for Mary, I believe we will see young women burst forth in lives of praise to God. And that is the goal of spiritual mothering."

DAY THREE

THE FAMILY OF GOD

*I*n his book *The Purpose Driven Life*, my pastor, Rick Warren, discusses God's family: "When we place our faith in Christ, God becomes our Father, we become his children, other believers become our brothers and sisters, and the church becomes our spiritual family. The family of God includes all believers in the past, the present, and the future."

ON YOUR OWN AND M&M'S

Q: Romans 12:10 in the Holman Christian Standard Bible (HCSB) speaks to Christian ethics: *"Show family affection to one another with brotherly love. Outdo one another in showing honor."* What do each of the following verses instruct us about our Christian family?
- Mark 3:33–35
- Galatians 6:10
- Ephesians 3:14–15
- Hebrews 2:11
- James 2:14–17
- 1 Peter 2:17
- 1 John 4:21

Q: How are we to treat our fellow brothers and sisters in Christ?

Q: How do you balance your personal family with your extended family in Christ?

- Do you give them equal time?

- Do you favor one more than the other?

- Do you feel guilty when you are with one family more than the other family? Additional thoughts?

M&M'S

Q: Discuss tips you have regarding balancing personal family with God's family (serving in ministry, at church, etc). If you are experiencing difficulty coordinating your calendars to meet, reread together the above Scriptures and discuss how to apply each of them to your scheduling dilemma.

FACE-TO-FACE REFLECTIONS

I read in our local newspaper a story about a secular comedian performing free shows in states hit hard by job losses. When asked what prompted him to do this, he answered, "We're all brothers and sisters." If the secular world understands we are family, how much more should Christians treat each other as such!

"Brother" and "sister," aren't said in the majority of churches today. It's unfortunate, because believers have the same Father, and we are family related by faith and Jesus's blood.

Many churches have small groups that function as mini-families. They meet, pray, eat, and do ministry together; care for each other's needs; support each other in crises; and celebrate victories. Maybe you are doing this study as part of such a small group.

I always say that mentoring is the smallest of small groups; it's two individuals meeting one-on-one, pouring into each other's life. That was God's plan for the preservation of the church: one generation would teach the next.

Family is not limited to church family; we are brothers and sisters with *all* believers in the family of God, and the Scriptures command us to be involved in each other's lives.

* * *

Mentoring Moment

"You are formed for God's family."—Pastor Rick Warren, *The Purpose Driven Life*

* * *

Day Four

Making Time for "Family"

lizabeth lived in *"a town in the hill country of Judah"* (Luke 1:39), which scholars believe were the hills surrounding Jerusalem. Most agree the distance between Mary and Elizabeth was somewhere between 50 to 100 miles. Mary apparently traveled by herself, probably on foot or at best on a donkey—in her first trimester of pregnancy.

On Your Own and M&M's

Q: Can you imagine Mary's trip? If you have experienced pregnancy or been around a pregnant woman, can you fathom a 100-mile journey as soon as you learned you were pregnant? What would your first thoughts be about such an adventure?

Q: What was going on in Elizabeth's life at this time?

● Yet, what did Elizabeth do when Mary arrived at her doorstep (Luke 1:41–45)?

Q: If you were in Elizabeth's position—elderly, six-months pregnant, in seclusion, husband unable to speak and thus out of work—and an unwed, pregnant, teenage, distant relative shows up unannounced, what would be your *first* response?

Q: What can we learn from Elizabeth and Mary about making time for relationships, even difficult or inconvenient ones?

Q: Are there areas of your life you could modify to make more time for relationships in your blood and Christian families?

M & M'S

Q: What changes can you make in your schedules to help you find more time to meet and possibly serve in ministry together?

• Discuss sacrifices you both are willing to make.

Q: How can you modify expectations that the setting you meet in must be perfect?

Q: What activities could you do together? For example, exercise is important, so how about taking a walk together or a gym class. List activities to discuss at your next meeting.

FACE-TO-FACE REFLECTIONS

Gabriel gave Mary a shocking message from the Lord. However, Mary also received the second part of the message that her elderly relative Elizabeth was in a similar circumstance, and that Mary would find comfort and reassurance in spending time with her. Gabriel's mention of Elizabeth compelled Mary to go to her immediately, no matter what the inconvenience, time required, energy expended, or sacrifice. Mary didn't stop to count the cost, consider the hardships of the travel, analyze if that was really what the Lord meant, worry about how it would affect her schedule, or wonder if Elizabeth was too old to relate to her.

Mary also didn't send a message to Elizabeth that Elizabeth should come visit her—after all, she was carrying the Messiah. No, Luke 1:39 says, *"Mary got ready and hurried"* to Elizabeth's house. Young Mary seemed to know that she needed the older Elizabeth, and that Elizabeth might have needed her.

From Elizabeth's response at Mary's arrival, it doesn't seem like Elizabeth worried or fretted that the house was a mess, or that she was out of coffee and cookies, or that she looked a sight and Zechariah really was not himself these days. She didn't tell Mary that there were a million things to do to get ready for her *own* baby, so this probably wasn't a good time for Mary's visit. She wasn't repulsed that her unwed, pregnant, teenage relative was on her doorstep. Instead, she joyfully welcomed Mary and they had a blessed reunion!

Today, our lives are so busy that we sometimes feel we don't have time to invest in true friendships and relationships. We fill our days with work, soccer games, church activities, house cleaning, shopping, errands—you know the routine. All good, necessary things. Yet how much of our day do we also fill with TV viewing, Internet browsing, and shopping for things we really don't need that cause us to work more to acquire and to maintain?

Mentors and mentees often complain that the hardest part of their relationship is finding time in their busy lives to meet, even though they know meeting would benefit them both. Others report that when they surrender their schedule to the Lord, He seems to give them more time and energy in their day to accomplish the things *He* knows are important. God does miracles in our relationships when we give Him the time.

PERSONAL PARABLE

When Kristen asked me to mentor her, it was an insanely hectic time in my life. I had a full-time career running an insurance agency, was a new wife and step-mom blending a family, and was working on a seminary degree. Where would I fit in time to mentor? And yet, I knew it was what God wanted, so I didn't hesitate to say yes when she asked me to mentor her. I often wonder what would have happened had I not fit Kristen into my life. Would I ever have started Woman to Woman Mentoring? Would God have continued to put "Kristens" in my life until I "got it"?

There are many testimonies from M&M'S who have taken the time to be in a mentoring relationship, and they all say they don't know how God does it, but He just makes more hours in their days. Maybe they go about their chores with more enthusiasm or decide some of the "to-dos" can wait. I feel like God puts an extra kick in my step and helps me accomplish all my tasks when I help Him with His family.

As I write this, I am at our mountain cabin, and across the street lives a young mom whose mother died several years ago and her dad died just last year. I feel this neighbor looks to me as a mentor and spiritual mother in her life. Even though I am often on deadline when I'm at the cabin, I know God wants me to take the time to be in her life. So I do. And as I focus on writing, this sweet young woman blesses me with firewood, or if I'm sick, brings homemade chicken soup, and watches over our cabin when we're not here.

Another neighbor back home is a young Christian mother. I walk with her every Saturday morning when I am home and she is available. During our walks she asks me questions like: How can I have a good marriage? When will I know my children are ready to be baptized? How do I answer my children's questions about what I did as a teenager? I don't have all the answers, but I can share with her from my experiences and God's biblical instructions. And that's all any mentor or spiritual mother need do. Extending yourself for the family of God is always a two-way blessing.

Mentoring Moment

We all have the same hours in a day,
but we don't have the same hours in a lifetime.

Face-to-Face with Elizabeth and Mary

DAY FIVE

A HUSBAND OF NOBLE CHARACTER. WHO CAN FIND?

oth Zechariah and Joseph were incredible husbands. The Bible doesn't tell us if the two men ever met, but I am sure that Elizabeth had many discussions with Mary about her upcoming wedding and being a wife. They probably also discussed how Mary would tell Joseph that she was pregnant.

ON YOUR OWN AND M&M'S

Q: How does Luke 1:5–6 describe Zechariah?

Q: What was Zechariah's ministry (Luke 1:8)?

Q: Based on Gabriel's words to Zechariah in Luke 1:13, what had Zechariah prayed for?

Q: Read Zechariah's Song in Luke 1:67–79. How was he able to prophesy so beautifully about his new son, John (v. 67)?

- What insight does this song give you into the kind of man Zechariah was?

Q: Read Matthew 1:18–19. Why was Joseph quietly going to divorce Mary?

- What changed his mind (Matthew 1:20–21)?

- How did Joseph respond to his angelic dream (Matthew 1:24)?

Q: How did Joseph show he was a man of honor and virtue (Matthew 1:25)?

Q: Tradition held that a first-born son was named after his father. Both Zechariah and Joseph named their sons according to Gabriel's instructions. What does this concession reveal about each man?

- How was breaking the naming protocol a witness to others (Luke 1:62–66; 2:21)?

ON YOUR OWN

Q: If you're married, describe your husband's noble characteristics.

Q: If you're not married, what noble characteristics might you look for in a husband?

- How can you let God be your husband for now?

M & M'S

Q: If one or both of you are married, describe to each other the noble characteristics of your husband.

Q: If one of you is not married, discuss noble characteristics in a prospective husband. Mentor, be sure that the first characteristic on the list is that he is a Christian, and discuss ways to let God be your "husband" in the meantime.

FACE-TO-FACE REFLECTIONS

Both Zechariah and Joseph were godly, understanding men. Zechariah's wife and Joseph's fiancée were experiencing unbelievably miraculous pregnancies, and yet, each man eventually accepted and acknowledged God's hand in both of the births.

During her visit with Elizabeth, Mary had the opportunity to observe a couple going through adversity, with Zechariah's loss of voice and Elizabeth's seclusion and very late-in-life pregnancy. I imagine Mary took note of how the elderly couple interacted, and she probably asked Elizabeth many questions about being pregnant and being a wife. The three months that Mary spent with Elizabeth and Zechariah prepared Mary to face Joseph when she returned home. And God had been preparing Joseph's heart to receive Mary and her unborn child.

PERSONAL PARABLE

When I was writing my book, *Dear God, They Say It's Cancer*, I was blessed to learn of men who stuck by their fiancées as they were going through breast cancer treatment. Many of these women had double mastectomies and lost all their hair from chemotherapy. But their men, who had professed undying love before cancer, proved to these brides-to-be that they were real men of integrity in the good and bad times. One young man even proposed to his fiancée *after* her cancer diagnosis.

A man of integrity who loves the Lord is good husband material. He will be able to weather the storms of adversity and ill health, as well as rejoice in the joys of marriage. Until you find that man, let God be your husband. Take it from me—a husband of noble character is well worth the wait and should be cherished as a gift from God.

Mentoring Moment

"For your Maker is your husband,
the LORD Almighty is his name
the Holy One of Israel is your Redeemer;
he is called the God of all the earth" (Isaiah 54:5).

FAITH IN ACTION

What one thing from this session does God want you to apply in your life today?

LET'S PRAY TOGETHER

Lord, we love our family and Your family. Help us to be loveable and available to any of them who are going through a tough time, and let us take the time to rejoice with those who are celebrating. Father, help us find the time to include others in our life, and when we need help, not to be afraid to ask others for assistance. Thank You that You are our Father who is in heaven. Amen.

WE ARE DIFFERENT

DAY ONE

THINGS IN COMMON,

AND NOT SO COMMON

Whatever the reasons, it is evident that young Mary sought out the company of the much older Elizabeth. She took the initiative and risk and quickly set out on the journey to Elizabeth's house. Mary must have felt that Elizabeth was a safe person and she would be welcomed in her home. Somehow, she knew she could go to Elizabeth with this wild story, and Elizabeth would understand. Often this kind of understanding and acceptance in mentoring relationships comes because the mentor has experienced some of the same things the mentee is going through, and the mentor is willing to be open and vulnerable in discussing them.

ON YOUR OWN AND M&M'S

Q: Even with the wide age difference between the two women, what are some things Elizabeth and Mary had in common?

- What are some differences between the two women?

- How did the commonalities overshadow any differences?

Q: What does 1 Corinthians 12:4–6 reveal about how we should view people who are different from us?

- 1 Corinthians 12:4 tells us that we might have different gifts, but we all have the same_____(fill in the blank).

- 1 Corinthians 12:5 says there are different kinds of service, but the same_____.

- 1 Corinthians 12:6 (NLT) instructs: God works in different ways, but it is the same _____who does the work in all of us.

Q: Have you ever taken the initiative to seek out a relationship with a significantly older or younger woman who seems a bit different than you?

- If so, describe the relationship?

- If not, what do you think is the value in such a relationship?

M & M'S

Q: What do the two of you have in common?

- If you can't think of anything now, come back and fill this in later in your relationship.

Q: What are some differences between the two of you?

Q: Discuss ways your commonalities and differences can complement each other. Make notes:

Elizabeth was further along in her pregnancy, so she could give Mary tips on what to expect as her own pregnancy progressed. Even though they were relatives from two different generations, seasons of life, and social circles, God graciously gave them a common bond of being chosen by Him to carry out a unique and history making assignment in a very common way for women — giving birth. Pregnancy was something they could both relate to, even though they were coming from a different perspective of age and experience. God can bridge generation gaps. While the women's individual mission for God seemed different, their lives, and their babies' lives, were intricately intertwined.

Their most strengthening common bond was their faith in God.

PERSONAL PARABLE

In the Woman to Woman Mentoring Ministry, we have experienced numerous incidences where M&M'S initially think they have nothing in common and cannot understand why they are matched together. As I listen to their delineation of why their lives seem so different from each other, I remind them that they have the only thing that really matters in common — Jesus Christ. I encourage them to start with that as a foundation and build from there.

The M&M'S usually respond with a kind of "aha" look. They confront the reality that they were looking for logistical similarities more than heart and spiritual commonalities.

Then months later these same M&M'S, who have matured together in their spiritual lives, often see the Lord's perfect plan revealed in a marriage saved, or a rift healed in a relationship, or parenting skills improved. There's always something that confirms to them that they were meant to be together.

Mentoring Moment

Even when there are no obvious similarities in our lives,
we can always celebrate and worship the Lord together
by studying His Word, praising Him, and enjoying
the eternal bond of everlasting life in Christ.

DAY TWO

HUSBAND AND WIFE DIFFERENCES

lizabeth had been married many years, and young, newly betrothed Mary probably had numerous questions about being a wife and homemaker.

Q: What do you think were some of the "marriage" questions that Mary asked Elizabeth?

• Why might these questions about marriage be easier to ask of a spiritual mother rather than her own mother?

Q: What premarital advice and counseling might Elizabeth give to Mary?

Q: What are some universal differences between men and women?

- Why do you perceive that God made men and women so different?

Q: How do the following verses help wives better understand how to support their husbands during trying and difficult times?
- Ephesians 5:22–24

- Colossians 3:18

Q: Conversely, how are husbands to support their wives, no matter what the circumstances?
- Ephesians 5:25–28

- Colossians 3:19

Q: The above Scriptures have been the source of much discussion. How do the Scriptures confirm that the husband and wife are to equally love and support each other?

ON YOUR OWN

Q: If you are single, who could give you wise counsel in choosing a godly mate and maintaining a Christ-centered marriage?

Q: If you are married, who needs you to share with her what you have learned about having a Christ-centered marriage?

M&M'S

Q: Mentor, if you are married, what lessons can you share about how to be a supportive wife?

• About how your husband supports you?

Q: Mentor, if you are married or single, share with your mentee how you've learned to deal with the differences between men and women.

Q: Mentee, if you are married or single, what questions do you have for your mentor about learning to celebrate differences between a husband and wife?

FACE-TO-FACE REFLECTIONS

Have you ever looked at a couple and thought, *I wonder what drew them together? What could they possibly have in common?* Maybe the husband or wife is much older than his/her spouse, or one is more attractive in some way than the other. One spouse might be better educated or refined, and you just don't get what one saw in the other, and yet, they seem very happy.

On the other hand, you and I both know couples who seem on the outside like they "go together," and yet they bicker and fight over everything.

God made men and women uniquely different. Women typically are more discerning and feeling-oriented, and men are generally more logical and action-oriented. There are always exceptions to the rule, but a couple that pleases the Lord will learn how to blend their differences into a relationship that honors God and shows others that with Christ at the center of their marriage, they can endure anything.

Mentoring Moment

Dare to be different by daring to overlook differences.

DAY THREE

WHEN YOU'RE SPIRITUALLY OLDER
THAN YOUR HUSBAND

echariah was a priest, and yet he initially doubted God's messenger. Joseph was a humble carpenter who wanted to do the right thing, which he thought was to quietly divorce Mary by signing legal papers to break the engagement.

ON YOUR OWN AND M&M'S

Q: Review Luke 1:5–6. *"In the time of Herod King of Judea"* informs us that they lived in a time of a wicked king's rule. Why would this be an important fact in describing Zechariah and Elizabeth?

• Elizabeth was not a priest, but how might her priestly heritage have affected her spiritual maturity?

Q: Who was Joseph a descendent of (Luke 1:27; 2:4), and why is this heritge significant (see Isaiah 9:1–7, 11–12)?

Q: How does the Bible describe Mary (Luke 1:27–28)?

Q: Read James 1:6. Contrast Zechariah's doubt with Elizabeth's faith (Luke 1:18, 25).

• Contrast Joseph's initial doubt (Matthew 1:19) with Mary's faith (Luke 1:38).

Q: Since Zechariah was a priest from a line of priests, thus a student of the Old Testament, what should have immediately come to his mind (Genesis 18:9–15)?

Q: Read Hebrews 12:10–11. Because of Zechariah's initial disbelief, God disciplined him (Luke 1:20). Why do even the righteous need discipline?

• Why do you think God chose the removal of Zechariah's voice as discipline?

• Without a voice, how could Zechariah communicate to Elizabeth what took place in the temple (Luke 1:22, 63)?

Q: Read 2 Corinthians 4:13. Why did Zechariah get his voice back, and how did discipline grow his faith (Luke 1:62–67)?

• Has God ever silenced you or your work because of your disbelief? Explain.

Q: We don't have a record of God reprimanding Elizabeth. Speculate how she may have reacted to Zechariah's story of the visit from the angel, and why he lost his voice.

Q: How do you think Elizabeth dealt with her priestly husband's temporary spiritual lapse?

Q: Mary probably didn't tell Joseph of her pregnancy immediately. She may have worried about how he would react. How could Elizabeth mentor Mary by sharing about Zechariah's doubt?

- How would this wise counsel help Mary deal with Joseph's initial reaction to divorce her (Matthew 1:18–19)?

- Who changed Joseph's mind (Matthew 1:20–21, 24–25)?

- How did Joseph's response to the angel display growing faith?

Q: If you are the more spiritually mature spouse in your marriage, what can you learn from Elizabeth and Mary about being a loving, patient wife?

Q: How does 1 Peter 3:1–2, 15–16 instruct the spiritually mature wife to treat her spiritually younger or unbelieving husband?

Q: How does 1 Peter 3:7 instruct husbands to treat their wives?

Q: Read 1 Corinthians 11:1. If you are married, how can you honor your husband as the head of your home, even if you are the more spiritually mature mate?

- If unmarried, what does it means to be the head of your home?

Q: Read 1 Corinthians 11:11. What have you learned from today's study about a husband-wife spiritual relationship?

M & M'S

Q: Mentor, if you're married, share with your mentee how you honor your husband as the head of your home. If this is an area you struggle with, ask your mentee to pray for you and keep you accountable. Share with her ways you would like to improve.

Q: Mentee, if your husband is not a believer, talk with your mentor about ways to model Christ and pray for him.

Q: If either of you is single, discuss ways to practically apply the Scriptures in marriages today.

FACE-TO-FACE REFLECTIONS

In Luke chapter one, both Zechariah and Mary questioned Gabriel. Walter Liefeld in *The Expositor's Bible Commentary* clarifies the context of the questions: Zechariah's question (v. 18) seems innocent, but v. 20 reveals that Zechariah was asking doubtfully. In contrast, Mary's question — "How can this be?" (v. 34) — arises from faith (v. 45). Mary simply inquired as to the way God would work, Zechariah questioned the truth of the revelation. "How can I be sure of this?" apparently was a request for a sign.

Zechariah's doubt did not erase his righteousness. He was human and therefore fallible. No one will reach perfection on earth. God disciplines us for our own good. It's important that wives not interfere with this process, but let God do His work in our husbands.

In *The One Year Walk with God Devotional*, Chris Tiegreen writes, "We view discipline as God's remedial recourse for a Christian who has gone far astray. But it is more universal than we like to think. It comes not only to those who have failed, but also to those whom God is preparing for greater success. It's what a father does for his children, and it's what our Father does for us."

Even though Zechariah was a priest, it seems that Elizabeth was more spiritually mature than her husband. And Mary initially showed more faith than Joseph. While Joseph wanted to do the right thing, we don't see him praying to God for guidance and wisdom. Sometimes wives are more intuitive to the Spirit, even though the husbands have more scholarly knowledge. It's often a case of heart versus head. Elizabeth set an excellent role model for Mary in how to be a loving, godly, patient wife when you are the more spiritually enlightened spouse. The result was that their husbands became believers in God's miracles.

* * *

Mentoring Moment

"Whenever a believer entertains doubts concerning God's word, he [she] loses his [her] testimony and his [her] song. Unbelief seals the lips, and they remain sealed until faith returns and bursts forth in praise and witness." —William MacDonald, *Believer's Bible Commentary*

DAY FOUR

ONE IS CHOSEN, ONE IS NOT

Mentoring/spiritual mothering often requires the mentor/ spiritual mother to decrease while the mentee increases.

ON YOUR OWN AND M&M'S

Q: When Mary entered the home of Zechariah and Elizabeth, what did she do first (Luke 1:40)?

- How did her greeting impact Elizabeth (Luke 1:41)?

- What insight did the Holy Spirit give to her (Luke 1:42–45)?

Q: Read Genesis 16:1, 29:31 and 1 Samuel 1:5–11. What did Sarah, Rachel, and Hannah have in common with Elizabeth?

Q: How might Elizabeth have been jealous of Mary (Genesis 30:1)?

- Read Proverbs 27:4. Why is jealousy worse than anger or fury?

- Read Romans 12:10. What can counter jealousy?

- Instead of jealousy, describe Elizabeth's emotion as she welcomed Mary (Luke 1:41–45).

Q: How did both women convey their humility (Luke 1:43, 48)?

Q: How would you have responded if you had been waiting years for a pregnancy, and then a young relative, who isn't even married, miraculously conceives?

Q: Parents often want their children to be the best and first in their class. How do you explain Elizabeth's joy that her child would not be the Messiah, but instead only pave the way for Him?

Q: Describe a time in your life when you were truly happy for someone selected over you for an honor.

- Was joy your initial response, like Elizabeth, or did you have to contemplate and pray about it?

Q: Think of a time when you were the one honored over someone else. Were you gracious and humble or prideful and boastful? If it was the latter, what have you learned from Mary to help you respond more graciously next time?

M & M'S

Q: Mentor, our goal as mentors is for our mentees to exceed us if possible—then we have really done our job and left a legacy. So encourage your mentee to be the best that she can be and don't feel threatened when she does exactly that.

Q: Discuss being sensitive to other people's feelings when you are chosen and they aren't.

FACE-TO-FACE REFLECTIONS

Mary humbly referred to herself as a *servant*. She didn't burst into Elizabeth and Zechariah's home, boasting and wanting to be treated as a royal guest. But the Holy Spirit had revealed Mary's good news to Elizabeth, who was honored that Mary came to her. Elizabeth displayed no pride, though she was of a priestly line, older, and wiser than Mary. Humbly, Elizabeth was subordinate to a teenager chosen to carry the Messiah—instead of Elizabeth herself, a godly woman who had waited so long for a baby. As a loving relative and spiritual mother, she was happy for her mentee's favor, not jealous or envious.

Every Jewish woman secretly hoped to be the mother of the Messiah. But Elizabeth had long since given up on being a mother at all, and now she was thrilled to be giving birth to a son who would be the forerunner of the long-awaited Messiah.

PERSONAL PARABLE

In the quest for the U.S. presidency, candidates often hurl verbal attacks at each other. Then losing candidates deliver humble concession speeches. However, the presidency pales in light of the Messiah's position. And never do we read of Elizabeth or Zechariah jockeying for position to let their son, John the Baptist, be the Messiah.

Mentoring Moment

"Not everyone willingly plays second fiddle,
but without a second, there is no first fiddle"
—Jill Briscoe

Day Five

What Will Others Think?

*M*ary saw value in spending time with Elizabeth, though Elizabeth was going through her own challenges.

On Your Own and M&M's

Q: Why do you think Elizabeth stayed in seclusion (Luke 1:24)?

Q: Read Genesis 30:22–23. What is the significance of Elizabeth's comment in Luke 1:25?

Q: Since Elizabeth's barrenness was disgraceful, what might her community have said about her pregnancy as an elderly woman?

- Do you think they considered her a freak of nature?

- What would have been your reaction?

Q: How might Elizabeth have advised Mary to handle embarrassing stares and hurtful comments?

Q: How would Joseph's acceptance of the pregnancy give Mary confidence?

Q: How much do you value what others think about you, and how does it influence your actions?

Q: With today's medical assistance, women can achieve pregnancy later in life. Have you been accepting or critical of this?

Q: Pray about how God could use you to make a difference in the lives of others different from you and going through a difficult time, then make plans to act on what the Holy Spirit reveals.

ON YOUR OWN

Q: Where in your community can you help women who are feeling shameful or disgraced?

M & M'S

Q: Is there a shelter for abused or homeless women, or pregnant teens, where you could serve together? Brainstorm ideas and make plans to follow through.

FACE-TO-FACE REFLECTIONS

After years of enduring infertility and its disgrace, Elizabeth now had the stigma of being an elderly pregnant woman. Can you see everyone pointing at Elizabeth and talking in hushed voices about the old wrinkled woman down the street who is pregnant, of all things! How could that happen? The Bible says that Elizabeth went into seclusion for five months (Luke 1:24). Maybe it was just too much for her. She was so joyful, and yet she had to feel uncomfortable under everyone's curious, scrutinizing glances.

Then Zechariah, a man of high honor and position—a priest no less—doubted God and lost his voice. More embarrassment. More speculation, gossiping, and finger-pointing. Add to that trying to prepare for a new baby when Zechariah and Elizabeth could only communicate through sign language or writing notes to each other.

Since Elizabeth was in seclusion, Zechariah had to go to the market, possibly facing more humiliation and ridicule. Zechariah was home (Luke 1:23) and probably on extended leave from his job after losing his voice. If your husband has ever been home from work for an extended period, you can relate to Elizabeth's plight.

Yet as different as Elizabeth's pregnancy was from the norm, it didn't top Mary's miraculous conception! When Mary returned home from visiting Elizabeth, she too would be subject to public scrutiny. Two miraculous pregnancies could cause quite a stir.

PERSONAL PARABLE

The family of former Alaska Governor Sarah Palin suddenly found themselves thrown into the public limelight when presidential candidate John McCain selected Palin to run on his ticket as vice president. Within days, the press released news that Sarah's 17-year-old unmarried daughter was pregnant, and for the next few weeks this teenager was the subject of media and tabloid scrutiny, ridicule, and gossip. The pregnancy received more press than the real issues of the campaign. I can only imagine what the press, if they had been around, would have done with the news of Elizabeth's and Mary's pregnancies.

* * *

Mentoring Moment

When you throw mud at someone,
you're the one who is losing ground.
—Anonymous

* * *

FAITH IN ACTION

What one thing from this session does God want you to apply in
your life today?

LET'S PRAY TOGETHER

*Lord, You created us all unique, and we will experience different
circumstances in our life. Please provide us with wisdom and guidance as to how we should lovingly respond to those who are different
from us. And for those of us who are married, help us to honor and
cherish our husbands regardless of their level of spiritual maturity
or shortcomings. Help us show love and kindness and not judge. If
we are the one being unfairly treated, show us the way to respond in
a manner that would be pleasing to You. Give us courage to pray for
our enemies. We need humility to prevail in a prideful world. Let it
start with us. Amen.*

SESSION FOUR
FACE-TO-FACE WITH ELIZABETH AND MARY:
GENERATION *to* GENERATION

MOTHER
KNOWS BEST

DAY ONE

FROM GENERATION TO GENERATION

*S*haring with the next generation some of what God has taught us is an honor and privilege. The blessing multiplies when the next generation is teachable.

ON YOUR OWN AND M&M'S

Q: What is the meaning of Mary's words in Luke 1:48–50?

• How does the next generation learn to revere God and live in harmony with His will?

Q: What do the following verses reveal about the significance of one generation passing down God's truths to the next, and the next generation's openness to those truths?

- Exodus 3:15
- Psalm 48:12–14
- Psalm 71:18
- Psalm 78:4
- Psalm 79:13
- Psalm 102:17

- Psalm 145:4–7
- Lamentations 5:19
- Daniel 4:3
- Luke 1:50
- Titus 2:1–8

Q: Now discuss how Elizabeth and Mary's relationship fulfilled the purpose of each passage.
- Exodus 3:15
- Psalm 48:12–14
- Psalm 71:18
- Psalm 78:4
- Psalm 79:13
- Psalm 102:17
- Psalm 145:4–7
- Lamentations 5:19
- Daniel 4:3
- Luke 1:50
- Titus 2:1–8
  (Specifically vv. 3–5)

Q: Next to the above verses, rate yourself using the following scale as to how you are fulfilling the intention of the Scripture:
- E–Effective
- N–Needs work
- M–Moderately effective

Q: In the areas where you rated yourself as moderately effective or in need of work, what are some immediate steps you could take to become effective? At the end of this study, return here to see what areas you have brought up to an E.

Q: If you were an E in every area, congratulations! How can you bump up your efforts to an S for Super Effective?

On Your Own

Q: If you are not in a mentoring relationship, in what other ways are you passing down, or preparing to pass down, to the next generation the lessons God has taught you?

Q: If you could not think of ways you are impacting the next generation for Christ, pray that God will reveal opportunities to you soon.

M & M'S

Q: A mentoring relationship is definitely a fulfillment of Titus 2:3–5. How do you see yourselves living out this Scripture passage?

Q: Discuss together how you rated yourselves in fulfilling the message of the other Scriptures and how you can become and E or S in all the areas.

FACE-TO-FACE REFLECTIONS

Throughout the Bible, God instructs one generation of believers to teach and train the next generation. Praise God, over the centuries believers have followed this mandate. Think of it: if they hadn't, you and I might not be Christians today! We are benefactors of the sacrifices of believers who have gone before us. Over the years, followers of God and His Son, Jesus Christ, have felt compelled to assure that the next generation:

● has access to the Bible and understands its contents
● knows how to communicate with God through the Holy Spirit and prayer
● receives guidance in leading a godly life

The question our generation must ask is: What is God calling believers—you and me—to do today? How can we invest our lives in the next generation, as Elizabeth did with Mary? Each of us must answer that question in a very personal and real way. If you are a mother, you are influencing the next generation through your children. A grandmother, your grandchildren. An employer, your employees. A ministry worker, the benefactors of your ministry. A pastor, your congregation. A schoolteacher, your students. A Sunday School teacher, the children in your classrooms every Sunday. A mentor, your mentee.

My rededication to the Lord in the summer of 1992 marked a turning point in my life. I moved from focusing on how I could further myself in this world to how could I further God's kingdom. When I prayed about what God was calling me to do, He clearly answered: I was to take a huge risk of leaving a well-paying career and go into full-time ministry. Not just any ministry—but a mentoring ministry that would develop and mature the next generations of believers. The rest is history, as my grandmother used to say.

*   *   *

Mentoring Moment

"When most people hear 'ministry,' they think of pastors, priests, and professional clergy, but God says every member of his family is a minister. In the Bible, the words *servant* and *minister* are synonyms, as are *service* and *ministry*. If you are a Chrsitian, you are a minister, and when you're serving you're ministering."
—Pastor Rick Warren, *The Purpose Driven Life*

Every believer, a minister.

*   *   *

DAY TWO

A TWO-WAY RELATIONSHIP

As is any healthy relationship, mentoring is always a two-way, reciprocal relationship. Elizabeth and Mary, though in different seasons of life, were perfect examples of reciprocity.

ON YOUR OWN AND M&M'S

Q: How do you see Elizabeth being a role model of Romans 5:3–5?

- Much of mentoring is sharing how God has helped you through the good, as well as the tough, times in life. How could Elizabeth's tough experiences be character building?

- What might Mary have learned from Elizabeth's role modeling?

- How could Mary apply lessons learned from Elizabeth?

Q: What are some practical household tips Elizabeth might have taught Mary?

Q: List ways Mary could have been a source of help and encouragement to Elizabeth.

Q: Explain a reciprocal relationship you've experienced where you helped each other.

M & M 'S

Q: Don't be surprised if, at times, the mentor mentee roles in your relationship switch. Has that happened yet? If so, explain.

Q: In what ways have you seen your mentoring relationship be reciprocal? Be ready to share this your next time together.

Q: Share a current area in your life where you could use the other one's help. Then commit to helping each other.

FACE-TO-FACE REFLECTIONS

When Mary arrived at her doorstep, Elizabeth probably was ready for some cheering up and someone to talk to, after enduring months of seclusion and her husband's silence. No wonder Elizabeth was joyful at first sight of her young relative Mary. The newness, freshness, energy, and awe of Mary's young innocence had to be contagious to the older Elizabeth, who was probably feeling pretty tired, fatigued, and lonely for female companionship. The excitement of Mary sharing the newness of her pregnancy and recent revelation from the Lord surely pepped up Elizabeth and gave her renewed purpose and strength.

Mary spent her first trimester with Elizabeth (Luke 1:56). Elizabeth helped Mary through those first sleepy morning sickness days. In turn, since Elizabeth was in her sixth month of pregnancy when Mary arrived, there is a good possibility that Mary helped with the birth of baby John. Often in a mentoring relationship, the mentee will assist the mentor through a stressful or difficult time or help celebrate a victory in her life. Mentors too need comfort, prayers, encouragement, assistance, and support, and it's a blessing when the mentee is sensitive to areas where she can give back to her mentor.

There is the misconception that to qualify as a mentor, a woman's life must be perfect and free from any distractions. We see that Elizabeth's life was far from that. We cannot put our lives on hold, or expect nothing out of the ordinary to happen, when we mentor. In fact, mentoring is about role modeling to a spiritually younger woman how a Christian woman faces the challenges of everyday life and willingly accepts help from others. Elizabeth certainly set that example for Mary.

The mentor often grows and matures spiritually along with the mentee as the mentor views her own life experiences differently and seeks out answers to the mentee's questions, or as they do a Bible study or read a book together. Healthy mentoring is never a hierarchy; it's always a two-way relationship.

PERSONAL PARABLE

We once had a mentor testify with a gleam in her eye that watching the enthusiasm and joyful excitement of young married love in her newlywed mentee made the mentor realize that she needed to add some spark back into her own 25-year marriage. Young mentees, or those young in the Lord, can help revive the original passion a more spiritually mature woman felt when her love for Christ was new.

Mentoring Moment

"The Chinese word for 'crisis' is a combination
of the characters meaning 'danger' and 'opportunity.'"
—*Daily Walk: Getting God's Word Into Your Heart*, April 8, 2009

DAY THREE

FILLED WITH THE SPIRIT

s soon as Elizabeth heard Mary's voice at the door, the Holy Spirit filled her and she began to prophesy about Mary and her baby (Luke 1:41). Elizabeth knew Mary's story immediately! Before Mary could even explain that she was carrying the blessed Messiah and had believed and trusted in the Lord, Elizabeth understood and was happy for her. Soon Mary was joyfully singing.

ON YOUR OWN AND M&M'S

Q: Read Luke 1:15, 41, 67. What was Elizabeth, Zechariah, and their unborn son, John filled with?

Q: Read Luke 2:25–27. When Mary and Joseph took baby Jesus to the temple, they met a devout man named Simeon who prophesied over Jesus. How did Simeon know about the baby?

Q: We talked in session one about the Holy Spirit in terms of the supernatural, but what does it mean to be *"filled with the Spirit"*? Use these verses to help answer this question:

- Exodus 31:1–3
- Deuteronomy 34:9
- Micah 3:8
- Acts 9:17–18
- Acts 13:52
- Ephesians 5:18

Q: Read Acts 2:36–40, 4:8–12, 24–32. How do we become filled with the Spirit?

Q: Read Romans 8:26–27 and Galatians 5:16–18. How does being filled with the Spirit help us to live godly lives?

Q: Read Galatians 5:22–23. What is the fruit of being filled with the Spirit?

Q: Read Galatians 5:25–26. How did being filled with the Spirit assist Elizabeth in her gracious and intuitive reception to Mary?

● How can being filled with the Spirit help you make wise choices and decisions?

Q: Why is it important to understand the Trinity — Father, Son, and Holy Spirit?

ON YOUR OWN

Q: Have you professed Jesus as your Savior and become a believer filled with the Holy Spirit?

● If you are not a believer and would like to make that decision for Christ and be filled with the Spirit, you can do that right now by praying the Salvation Prayer that follows.

● If you just accepted Christ into your heart, find a mentor who will disciple you and help you mature in your new faith.

● If you still have questions about accepting Christ into your heart, seek out a believer who will talk and pray with you.

M & M'S

Q: Mentee, are you a believer? If the answer is yes, then ask your mentor any questions you have about being *"filled with the Spirit"* and how the Holy Spirit works in a believer's life every day.

- If the answer is no, would you like to accept Jesus into your heart right now by personally believing in Him and receiving eternal life? I hope so. You can pray the Salvation Prayer below on your own or with your mentor. I know your mentor would love to pray this prayer with you.

- Mentor, if your mentee is a new Christian, your relationship should be focused on discipling her and helping her grow and mature in her faith. The "Face-to-Face" Bible studies are designed to assist you in this privileged role.

SALVATION PRAYER

Dear Jesus, I know that I have sinned in my life, and I want to tell You how sorry I am. I ask You now to forgive me and cleanse me of those sins. Jesus, I want You to come into my heart and take residence there. I believe You are the Son of God and that You died on the cross to pay the price for my sins and then rose again in three days to offer me eternal life. Jesus, I give You complete control of my life, and I willingly surrender my heart, mind, and soul to You. Please fill me with the Holy Spirit and Your love. Lord, I give You my life—make me a new creation in You. In Your Son Jesus's name, I pray. Amen.

If you prayed the Salvation Prayer: Welcome to the family of God! God just wiped away your past sins, and you have a new slate: a new life in Christ. Congratulations! Celebrate and tell others about the decision you just made to become a follower of Jesus Christ—it's your testimony. Now you are ready to grow and mature spiritually, and this study will have so much more meaning to you. You go, girl!

When Jesus ascended back to heaven, He left the Holy Spirit to intercede for us and to be our Counselor and Comforter. Prior to Jesus's ascension, Spirit-filled prophets testified about people's lives, as Simeon did with Jesus, and even Zechariah and Elizabeth prophesied. I think it's easy for us to forget sometimes that there is a trinity—Father, Son, and Holy Spirit, and we can speak directly to the Holy Spirit and He speaks to us, through prayer and God's Word. We don't need prophets or interpreters, we just need to open our hearts and our souls and let the two-way communication begin.

PERSONAL PARABLE

We all receive the Holy Spirit the day we become Christians, but living our daily life "filled with the Spirit" can be a challenge. I know that the challenges of this world drain me, and at the end of the day—or maybe even in the middle of the day—I'm not feeling very Spirit-filled in my thoughts or actions. That's why *every* morning in my quiet time I ask God to fill me with the Holy Spirit. I also pray that His work is done in my earthly life as it is in heaven. Sometimes, I have to stop and pray this prayer several times throughout the day. The sign that I'm in need of a Holy Spirit refill is when I become critical, anxious, snappy, judgmental—everything that is the opposite of the fruit of the Spirit.

Mentoring Moment

"To be filled with the Holy Spirit is to be filled with Christ. The Holy Spirit came to glorify Christ. Therefore, if I am filled with the Spirit, I am abiding in Christ…And if I am controlled and empowered by Christ, He will be walking around in my body, living His resurrection life in and through me."—Bill Bright

DAY FOUR

AN ENCOURAGING WORD

lizabeth's Holy Spirit-inspired greeting encouraged Mary. What an affirmation for Mary to hear a relative cheering her on, when she had a doubting fiancé and perhaps an ashamed family. Instead of being worried or troubled, Mary's heart filled with joy as she trusted God and responded back to Elizabeth with a Spirit-filled hymn of praise.

ON YOUR OWN AND M&M'S

Q: Next to each of the following Scriptures, write how it applies to Elizabeth and Mary's initial exchange of words (Luke 1:39–55):
- Job 16:5
- Romans 1:11–12
- 1 Corinthians 14:3
- Ephesians 4:15
- Colossians 2:2–3
- 1 Thessalonians 2:7–8,12
- 1 Thessalonians 4:18
- 1 Thessalonians 5:11

Q: Words build up or tear down. Describe the power James ascribes to our words in James 3:5–12.

- Who can tame our tongue to use it for good (James 3:13, 17–18, 4:7)?

Q: Describe a time when someone's kind, encouraging words and actions helped you through a difficult or stressful time in life.

- Have you thanked this person for his/her encouragement? If not, send them a note or make a phone call.

Q: Have you offered encouragement to someone in a compromising or tough spot? Tell how you found the right words to say and actions to take. Tell how it helped them.

M & M'S

Q: Mentor, offer your mentee some encouraging words of affirmation regarding steps you see she is taking to be a godly woman. Make notes here.

Q: Mentee, let your mentor know areas where you could use encouragement as you develop your spiritual life as a woman. Make notes here.

- Remember your mentor could use encouragement too!

Q: What are some ways a mentor can help her mentee discern what God's plans and purposes might be for her?

FACE-TO-FACE REFLECTIONS

Harvey Mackay writes a newspaper column called "Lessons in Leadership." Once he discussed a study of two literary groups at the University of Wisconsin. The men's group called themselves the Stranglers: "They were heartless, tough, even mean in their criticism." The women's group was the Wranglers: "The criticism was much softer, more positive, more encouraging." Twenty years later, not one of the Stranglers had a literary accomplishment, but the Wranglers had produced six or more successful writers including Marjorie Kinnan Rawlings who wrote *The Yearling*. The conclusion: "The Wranglers highlighted the best, not the worst."

A mentor/spiritual mother should be like the Wranglers: a cheerleader encouraging the things her mentee is doing that please God. Many people fear the word *mentor* because they think it means disciplinarian. But mentoring is more than guiding a mentee in making corrections and changes; it's helping her discover and build on God's purpose and plans for her. One way to do that is with words that sincerely edify, confirm, bolster, build up, counsel, bless, and direct in love.

Each generation hungers for affirmation and encouragement from mature people they admire. Young women need to know they matter to God and to us.

PERSONAL PARABLE

My sister went to visit my daughter Kim, and as the family sat together, two-year-old Katelyn announced that three-year-old Brandon wasn't going to get a treat after dinner because he hadn't finished his food. My sister commented on Kim's parenting; Kim braced herself, thinking, *Oh, what am I doing wrong?* But my sister assured Kim that she was complimenting her because it was apparent the kids knew the consequences of unsatisfactory behavior. Kim said she let out a sigh of relief and was so encouraged that she was a better mom than she thought she was.

Mentoring Moment

"For every critical comment we receive,
it takes nine affirming comments to even out the
negative effect in our life." —Jim Burns

Face-to-Face with Elizabeth and Mary

Day Five

Judgment or Discernment?

We have the advantage of knowing the end of the story of how God fulfilled His plans for John the Baptist and Jesus. But consider that their parents were relying strictly on what the angel Gabriel said, and no one around them was privy to that same celestial encounter. What a true test of relationships with friends and relatives, who might have thought them crazy. But those who believed their stories witnessed the mighty and miraculous work of the Lord.

On Your Own and M&M's

Q: What were the people outside the temple doing while they waited for Zechariah to come out (Luke 1:10)?

• As a result, what was the reaction of the bystanders when Zechariah emerged (Luke 1:22)?

Q: In Luke 1:58, why were the neighbors and relatives joyful over Elizabeth's baby?

• How did they react when Zechariah's voice returned (Luke 1:65–66)?

Q: Read Luke 2:36–38. What had the prophetess, Anna, been doing while she awaited the birth of Jesus?

Q: What common theme do you observe in the people who understood and accepted that God was working through Elizabeth and Zechariah and Mary and Joseph?

Q: Read Matthew 7:1–5. What should you do first before you criticize or judge someone—especially a fellow believer?

Q: Paraphrase Proverbs 10:19–21 as a definition of foolish judgment versus righteous discernment:

Q: Read Romans 12:2–3. What does the *"renewing of your mind"* mean?

- How would a renewed mind help determine judgment versus discernment?

- What helps you determine if you are being judgmental or discerning?

- How could you become a more discerning person?

Q: Evaluate your usual reaction to a generation that is different from yours (older and younger). Are you: critical, judgmental, understanding, tolerant?

- How would a renewed mind that looked for the best in people, help you be more understanding and accepting of the ways of different generations?

       Face-to-Face with Elizabeth and Mary

- What can you do to renew your mind?

Q: How would you have reacted to Elizabeth's story? Mary's story? Be honest and write what you think would be your first:
- Response —
- Thoughts —
- Words —
- Actions —

ON YOUR OWN

Q: If you struggle with being critical and judgmental, it would help to have an accountability partner. Consider who you could ask to help you become more discerning.

M & M'S

Q: Discuss together your answers to the question regarding how you would have reacted to Elizabeth's story and Mary's story.

Q: Have you told each other your life story? If not, do that now. But first stop and pray that you will be receptive to what the other woman has to tell you.

- If you have already learned about each other's life, talk now about how you received some of the information. Ask forgiveness if you were judgmental or disbelieving.

Q: Discuss ways to keep each other accountable in being less critical and judgmental of others.

FACE-TO-FACE REFLECTIONS

Did you answer the question about reacting to Elizabeth and Mary: I would have prayed for the Holy Spirit to give me wisdom and discernment? If that was your first thought, congratulations —you probably would have responded to Mary the same way

Elizabeth did. But for many of us, that would not have been our first response. We might have judged rather than discerned—thought the worst before considering the best.

Connie Culp, who received the first face transplant in the United States after her husband shot her in the face, gives wise advice: "When somebody has a disfigurement and doesn't look as pretty as you do, don't *judge* them, because you never know what happened to them." Elizabeth's and Mary's situations are a good example of waiting until you have the whole story and a word from God before you react.

The way I determine between healthy discernment and being judgmental is whether I'm operating with a critical or condemning spirit. I'm being judgmental if I'm thinking negative, unkind, critical thoughts such as: *I'm better than they are. How could they? I wouldn't have done that. They are Christians, they should know better than that.* Or even, *I wonder if they are Christians, the way they act.* Being judgmental stems from our own self-righteous and self-centered perceptions, opinions, and thoughts.

Discernment stems from love: the fruit of the Spirit. If God reveals to us something through prayer, His Word, a sermon or message, or even through our thought life, He also will give us appropriate words and actions to deal with it. Scripture always validates discernment.

If discerning thoughts are from the Holy Spirit, where do you think harmful, judgmental thoughts come from? Satan. He puts those thoughts on our minds, and he wins when we act on them.

As a mentor/spiritual mother, your mentee may present you with a tough situation or she may do something you don't agree with. Two questions to ask yourself before approaching her are: "What is my motivation?" and "Is my perspective in agreement with God's perspective?" You'll find the answers to these two questions through prayer, reading God's Word, asking questions of your mentee, and seeking wise council before approaching her. Then remember that God tells us to speak the truth in love.

Some mentees will need an accountability partner to help them resist temptation, addiction, bad habits, or any area of struggle. It's important that the mentee first identify the area where she needs accountability. Then, she formally needs to give the mentor permission to keep her accountable in the problem area. Next,

M&M'S must discuss ways to accomplish this goal that are agreeable to both of them. For more on accountability relationships see the *Woman to Woman Mentoring Mentor* and *Mentee Handbooks*.

PERSONAL PARABLE

In *Praying for Your Prodigal Daughter*, I discuss a conversation I had with my former prodigal daughter, Kim, when she was contemplating making a full commitment to Christ and being baptized. Kim asked me questions: what would her friends think and would she still be able to have fun? As she answered her own questions before I could open my mouth, she suddenly said, "And I guess I'll have to give up my critical spirit that says sarcastically: Hey check out what that dude is wearing!" As a new believer, Kim knew that thinking the worst of people before she thought the best would have to change in her life.

I am sure that Kim received some of that critical spirit from me. I used to have a pretty quick tongue, and it is something I have to pray about all the time. But isn't that the answer to all our faults? We can't do any of this on our own. Just like Elizabeth and Mary needed the prompting and support of the Holy Spirit, so do we; and praise the Lord, He is just waiting for us to call on Him!

Mentoring Moment

"When we don't like someone,
it's easy to attribute all their actions—
even good ones—to bad motives. When we like someone, we tend to excuse their wrong actions by saying that they have a good heart. Both responses—falsely condemning and falsely excusing actions—are judgmental." — Pastor Tom Holladay, *The Relationship Principles of Jesus*

FAITH IN ACTION

What one thing from this session does God want you to apply in your life today?

LET'S PRAY TOGETHER

Lord, You made us to be in community and to participate in each other's lives. We pray that we would be encouragers, and that we would pass down to the next generation both the hard lessons we have learned and the joys and blessings that come from giving our heart and life to You. Help us to be discerning of those in our family and in our lives who could benefit from the wisdom and experience that comes from years of walking in this world and walking with You. Give us the words and discernment to reach the next generation for Christ. Help us to be tolerant and understanding of people who are older and younger than us. In Jesus name we pray. Amen.

SESSION FIVE
FACE-TO-FACE WITH ELIZABETH AND MARY:
GENERATION *to* GENERATION

WORSHIPPING
TOGETHER

DAY ONE

A SPIRITUAL RELATIONSHIP

lizabeth was truly the epitome of a spiritual role model, and Mary responded in kind.

ON YOUR OWN AND M&M'S

Q: Identify spiritual attributes you observed in Elizabeth.

- Why are these good attributes for a mentor?

- How might Elizabeth have used these spiritual attributes to disciple the spiritually younger Mary?

Q: Describe how Mary matured spiritually from the naïve "hand-maid" visited by Gabriel to the spiritually insightful young woman who gave the worshipful, prophetic response to Eliza-beth's greeting. (Compare Luke 1:28–29 with Luke 1:46–55).

Q: Read Proverbs 18:6–8. With everything going on in both their lives, what might have Elizabeth and Mary spent time doing when they first saw each other?

- Instead, how did Elizabeth and Mary worship together, according to Psalm 100:2?

Q: Read Romans 12:1. How is sacrifice a form of worship?

- Explain how Elizabeth and Mary lived out this verse.

Q: What sacrifices are you willing to make that would please God?

ON YOUR OWN

Q: Which of Elizabeth's spiritual attributes do you see in yourself?

- How could you use these attributes to mentor someone?

- Stay alert to who God might put in your life to mentor.

M & M'S

Q: Mentor, at which of Elizabeth's spiritual attributes do you excel, and where do you need work?

- How will this make you a better mentor?

Q: Mentee, what did you learn from Mary's spiritual growth?

- What can you do to contribute to worship in your meetings?

Q: How do the two of you exemplify Psalm 100:2 in your time together?

Q: Talk about ways to keep your time with each other focused on the Lord and His will for your life. Make some notes here:

Q: What will you do each time you meet to insure that you keep God at the center of your relationship and meetings?

Q: Agree to keep each other accountable about not gossiping when you are together. How will you do that? (Reread together the discussion on accountability partners on pages 90–91).

FACE-TO-FACE REFLECTIONS

Mary must have been overjoyed as she listened to the admired and respected Elizabeth confirm that she, Mary, was blessed indeed: "*What the Lord has said to her will be accomplished!*" (Luke 1:45). Here was a spiritually and chronologically older woman telling Mary that great things were going to happen in her life because the Lord said so! Mary responded enthusiastically and broke into singing her Magnificat in Luke 1:46–56. Their initial meeting was an amazing time of praise and worship.

Notice, they did not start immediately discussing what was happening in their lives or gossiping about how their husband and fiancé were such doubting men—while they were so much more spiritually mature. Nor did they lament their wrongful treatment as outcasts due to the unusual happenings in their lives. There was no: Poor me. Why me? I can't believe this is happening to me! I'm so depressed and tired. Or I'm so_____(fill in the blank). If we are not careful, that often is how our mentoring sessions, or girlfriend times, can begin. We babble and chat—then babble and chat some more—maybe complain a bit and even gossip. Suddenly, it's time to go and we never even brought up the Lord's name, not to mention cracked open our Bibles.

Elizabeth and Mary started their time together in worshipful praises, song, and exclamations of their bountiful blessings. Right from the beginning, they gave all the honor and glory to God. Mary participated in this time too. She didn't leave all the spiritual talk to Elizabeth, but instead shared what she knew of the wonderful and great things the Lord had done for her. No matter how new we are in our spiritual walk, we can always give thanks to the Lord that He is in our life.

PERSONAL PARABLE

I have a friend who loves to sing praises, pray, and worship the Lord whenever we get together. When we first met socially as couples, she would halt the chitchat and ask what was going on in our life that needed prayer. The first time she did this, I'll admit I was a little surprised. It wasn't that I don't like to pray, but we were spending a relaxing time getting to know each other, and it was clear she felt that was a waste of our precious time. Now prayer has become such a regular part of our time together that, when she doesn't break out in prayer, I do.

It's so refreshing to have friends in our life who care what is happening with us spiritually and personally.

Mentoring Moment

"I am going to say something to you which will sound strange. It even sounds strange to me as I say it, because we are not used to hearing it within our Christian fellowships. We are saved to worship God. All that Christ has done for us in the past and all that He is doing now leads to this one end." —A. W. Tozer

DAY TWO

NOTHING IS IMPOSSIBLE WITH GOD

lizabeth and Mary both experienced nothing short of a miracle. Neither woman's pregnancy could have occurred the way it did by any of their own efforts. If either of their scenarios happened today, would we call it fantasy? Impossible? A delusion? Or would we proclaim a miracle?

ON YOUR OWN AND M&M'S

Q: How did Gabriel explain to Mary the "impossible" happening in both her and Elizabeth's life (Luke 1:37)?

Q: How does each of the following verses explain seemingly "impossible" circumstances in a believer's life?
- Jeremiah 29:11
- Matthew 17:20
- Matthew 19:26
- Mark 10:27
- Luke 18:27

Q: Read Hebrews 11:6. What does a believer have to possess in order to see God in the impossible?

Q: When Zechariah emerged from the temple with no voice, what was the reaction of the people who were waiting outside for him (Luke 1:22)?

● What was the neighbor's reaction when Zechariah's voice returned (Luke 1:65–66)?

Q: How did Elizabeth's neighbors and relatives respond when they learned that Elizabeth had a baby (Luke 1:58)?

● What prophecy did this fulfill (Luke 1:14)?

Q: What's God's purpose in publicly performing the "impossible"?

Q: What helps you trust in God during impossible circumstances?

Q: Describe a time in your life where something was humanly impossible but God intervened and the impossible became possible.

● Did you remember to give God the glory? Explain.

● Were others watching this miracle take place, and did they give God the glory? Explain.

Q: What current situation in your life seems impossible?

● Are you discouraged or have you given the situation over to God to handle? Discuss your answer.

ON YOUR OWN

Q: It's never easy going through a stressful time on your own. If currently you are experiencing discouragement with an impossible situation, I know you would find solace in seeking out another woman who has been in your shoes. Will you do that soon?

Q: Or if God has seen you through an impossible situation, who could benefit from the wisdom you learned? When will you seek out someone to mentor through a difficult time? Make a commitment here:

M & M'S

Q: What situation in your lives needs a divine intervention? Share with each other a difficult circumstance, and then pray and watch as God unfolds His plan. Be sure to journal the results in the Prayer & Praise Journal pages that begin at page 139, and remember that everything happens in God's timing.
● Mentor, take responsibility for continually turning challenging circumstances over to God whenever one of you wants to take the control back into your own hands.

FACE-TO-FACE REFLECTIONS

Our God specializes in doing the impossible. Nothing is impossible for God—only our finite mind makes the possible look impossible. The foundation of our faith is trust—trusting that a good God has our best interests in mind. But many times we actually trust humans to do the impossible more than we trust God! Is our first thought when an illness strikes, *God could heal me*, or do we put more faith in the doctor? When our finances are dismal, do we seek the advice of a financial planner first, or do we go to God with our concerns? When our marriage is in trouble, do we think only a marriage counselor could fix it, or do we rely more on our heavenly Counselor?

Not to say that doctors, financial planners, and counselors are not here to help us, but not one of them can turn an impossible situation into the possible without God's intervention. Stop and think about that statement for a moment: no human being can do the impossible. No matter how much he or she thinks it is by his or her power, it is not.

When we stop putting our trust in humans and start *blamelessly* trusting God, we can count on seeing the impossible turn to the possible in our life, just like Zechariah and Elizabeth and Mary and Joseph. But remember that the possible may not be what we were planning. Mary certainly never planned on a divine conception, but you and I are Christians today because she trusted God to do the impossible.

PERSONAL PARABLE

Every writer, speaker, and preacher will admit that the Lord has him or her write about things they need to work on in their own life, and I am no exception. Today as I write to you, our country has plummeted into a terrible recession and my husband and I find that our retirement fund plummeted with the economy. We no longer have years for it to rebound. We are closer to retirement than we are far from it.

Our situation to the outside eye looks impossible. All our best laid plans and following the financial world's rules have failed. Yet we know the plans the Lord has for us are not for ruin, but instead, He promises to give us hope and a future. However, there is one thing He does ask of us in order to benefit from this promise—we must have faith.

Some day soon, I know that I will be writing about how the Lord turned our impossible financial situation into our possible retirement. Our job is to be blameless and faithful in our prayers and publicly to give God all the glory for our rescue.

Mentoring Moment

When there is nothing left but God,
we discover that God is all we need.

DAY THREE

LISTENING TO GOD

*I*n the biblical story we have been studying, we hear God's voice through His messenger, the angel Gabriel.

ON YOUR OWN AND M&M'S

Locate every verse in Luke chapter one where the angel Gabriel is speaking to someone, and note whether the recipient acknowledged hearing the angel's voice.

Q: Read these verses, and note what Scripture says about listening:
- Psalm 34:2
- Proverbs 1:5
- Proverbs 8:32–34
- Proverbs 18:13
- Proverbs 22:17–18
- Isaiah 28:23
- James 1:19

Q: In Luke 1:18, how did Zechariah fail to heed the advice in Proverbs 18:13 and James 1:19?

Q: How do we know that even though Zechariah spoke without completely listening, He did hear what the angel instructed (Luke 1:62–63)?

Q: In Mary's encounter with Gabriel in Luke 1:28–38, how does Mary apply Proverbs 22:17? (Note: Luke 1:46–55.)

Q: Read Luke 3:16 and John 14:15–19, 26. Today, it would be rare to have angels speaking directly to us, but who is God's voice to believers?

* How aware are you of the Holy Spirit communicating with you?

Q: Read Psalm 46:10. What must you do to hear God?

Q: Read Psalm 119:11 and John 1:1. What other ways does God use to speak to us?

* How does God speak to you?

* Do you listen to His promptings? Give an example.

Q: How would having regular quiet time help you hear God better?

* How is a quiet time a form of worship?

M & M'S

Q: Share experiences of God speaking into your life and the results of either listening or not listening.

Q: Mentee, if you are not clear on how the Holy Spirit speaks to us today, consider doing a study on the Holy Spirit when you finish this study.

Q: Keep each other accountable to having a daily quiet time and listening to God.

Luke 1:31 reads: *"Now __listen__: You will conceive and give birth to a son, and you will call His name JESUS"* (HCSB, with emphasis added). We know that Gabriel got Mary's attention and she listened and obeyed.

Luke 1:20 (HCSB) says, *"Now __listen__! You will become silent and unable to speak"* (emphasis added). Gabriel was telling Zechariah that because he asked for a sign to verify the "good news" Gabriel brought him, and spoke before he listened to everything the angel had to say, Zechariah would loose his ability to speak until his baby was born. Zechariah certainly had to do a lot of listening over the next nine months. Elizabeth might have actually been thrilled, because the major complaint most wives have is that their husband's don't listen to them when they speak. I know that's an ongoing issue with Dave and me.

Imagine if you couldn't speak for nine months! What a perfect opportunity to listen to the Lord. However, you don't have to live in silence to clearly hear God; you just need to be aware of when He is speaking. You may not hear an audible voice, but you will sense the Holy Spirit nudging your heart and mind as you:

- read your Bible
- pray
- listen to a sermon, teaching, or worship music
- journal
- just go about your day.

God also often speaks to us through other believers. When He wants to tell you something, He *will* get your attention. Expect it!

I often retreat to our cabin in the mountains to write, where there is no one to talk to except the morning and evening phone call from my husband and the occasional neighbor or squirrel I meet while out walking. I hear the Lord so clearly when I am silent before Him. It feels like I am in a continual conversation with the Holy Spirit. I often comment that it's as if I have a direct line to the Lord, and He to me, when I'm at this silent retreat.

But I am aware of the Holy Spirit talking to me at other times too. I often feel like I'm having a conversation with myself, then it hits me — I'm talking to the Holy Spirit! For example, when the Holy Spirit prompted me to "feed My sheep," I thought someone else was talking to me. I'm so glad I listened, prayed, and discovered it was the Holy Spirit's call to start the Woman to Woman Mentoring Ministry. I didn't know at first that God was calling me to start the ministry, but as I continued to respond to His promptings, the Holy Spirit continued to show me the way I should go.

In my daily life, the Holy Spirit prompts me to send an email, card, or call someone; or reminds me of something I have forgotten to do; or gives me an idea to write about; or protects me from some unforeseen harm. Consequently, I find myself saying throughout the day: "Thank You, God."

Mentoring Moment

God gave us two ears and one mouth
so that we can listen twice as much as we speak!

DAY FOUR

OUR PRAYERS ARE HEARD.
PRAISE GOD!

The name Zechariah means "The Lord remembers." Elizabeth and Zechariah had been praying for many years for a baby, and even though they may have given up on that request, God hadn't.

ON YOUR OWN AND M & M'S

Q: What did the angel say to Zechariah in Luke 1:13?

• How long do you think it had been since Elizabeth and Zechariah had prayed for a child?

Q: When does the angel say this birth will take place (Luke 1:20)?

Q: Read 1 Chronicles 5:20. What does the awaited answer to prayer tell us about Zechariah and Elizabeth's faithful trust in God?

Q: Read Hebrews 6:10–12. How do you see God rewarding Zechariah and Elizabeth's patience?

Q: Who does Elizabeth acknowledge and give glory to for her "unplanned pregnancy" (Luke 1:25)?

Q: Reread Luke 1:13–17, 68–79. How does Zechariah confirm that he understands why they had to wait for their prayers for a baby to be answered?

- Who gave this revelation to Zechariah?

Q: How would Mary's visit help confirm to Elizabeth and Zechariah the future role of their baby (Luke 1: 14–17)?

Q: Compare Elizabeth's praise in Luke 1:25 to Mary's praise song in Luke 1:46–49.

Q: Read Ephesians 1:11–13. How are we to praise God for His plans for our life?

Q: Rate yourself in patiently waiting for God's timing in answering prayer, by selecting from the following options:
- Extremely patient and long-suffering
- Moderately patient, but a little anxious
- Not patient, full of anxiety

Q: What do these verses tell us about anxiety?
- Psalm 139:23
- Proverbs 12:25

Q: Read Philippians 4:6. What does the Bible tell us is the antidote to anxiety?

Q: Personalize Mary's Magnificat. Write your own lyric of praise and joy to the Lord for what you have seen Him do in others' lives and in yours.

ON YOUR OWN

Q: Read Ecclesiastes 4:9–12. Elizabeth had Zechariah while she waited for answered prayer and Mary had Elizabeth to confide in. Do you have someone to wait with you? If not, ask God to bring an M&M into your life. How about writing that request in your Prayer & Praise Journal that begins on page 139.

M&M'S

Q: You are so fortunate to have each other. Be sure you are sharing prayer requests and noting how and when God answers. Take a moment right now to update your Prayer & Praise Journals together. Remember to open and close your times together in prayer; maybe even include some praise music.

FACE-TO-FACE REFLECTIONS

It's doubtful that when Gabriel said to Zechariah, *"your prayer has been heard,"* that Zechariah was at that moment praying for a child. I am sure Gabriel's announcement that they would have a son caught Zechariah by complete surprise. Since Zechariah and Elizabeth were elderly, we can assume that they had stopped praying for a child a long time ago. And yet, Elizabeth immediately recognized that this child was a long-awaited answer to prayer. Elizabeth knew her blessing came from God.

Chris Tiegreen reminds us on May 12 of *The One Year Walk with God Devotional*:

The call of Scripture is contrary to our natural inclination. We are called to believe God with reckless abandon—not just believe that He is there and that He is involved with us somehow, though we're not sure exactly how; but that He is actively, personally seeking our good and answering our prayers. We are to give up our own strategies and ambitions, to relinquish all "Plan Bs." To recklessly, irrevocably cast ourselves completely into His arms.

Zechariah, Elizabeth, Mary, and Joseph did what is so hard for us to do—they trusted God completely with "reckless abandon." It's scary, but if you truly believe that God has your best interest in mind, you will pray and expectantly wait—because really—has God ever let you down?

PERSONAL PARABLE

Have you ever prayed for something and then forgot about it? I have, so I'm passionate about keeping a prayer and praise journal. Writing down prayer requests, and then noting when God answers, keeps you in a continual state of worshipful praise and giving God the glory He deserves.

In my book, *Praying for Your Prodigal Daughter*, I chronicle five years of praying for my daughter Kim to come to know the Lord and change her wayward ways. Daily I prayed, and daily I journaled. Periodically I would review my prayer requests and note the answered prayers, which encouraged me through the years when I saw no change in her.

Looking back at my journal as I wrote the book, I saw answers to prayers that I had forgotten journaling. Through my prayer and praise journal, I clearly saw God's hand in my daughter's life, as I persistently prayed, even when my heart was aching and there was no improvement. Writing our prayer requests allows us to see God at work, because as we all know, He may not be quick to answer and our memories can be very short.

Mentoring Moment

"If the request is wrong, God says: *No*
If the timing is wrong, God says: *Slow*
If you are wrong, God says, *Grow*
But if the request is right, the timing is right, and you are right,
God says: *Go!*"—Pastor Bill Hybels, *Too Busy Not to Pray*

DAY FIVE

LIFE INVESTMENT

*S*piritual mothering involves investing time and energy into a spiritually and chronologically younger woman. This investment will always pay high dividends in your heavenly account.

ON YOUR OWN AND M&M'S

Q: Read the parable of the talents in Matthew 25:14–30. How does this parable apply to mentoring?

● How does the parable apply to Elizabeth's investment in Mary?

Q: What was Elizabeth's initial response to the opportunity placed before her to be a spiritual mother to Mary (Luke 1:43)?

Q: What was her first spiritual investment in Mary (Luke 1:45)?

● What was the immediate return on her "investment" (Luke 1:46–55)?

Q: Based on their initial greeting, what can you speculate was the depth of their spiritual relationship during the next three months?

Q: What divine insight did Elizabeth learn from her husband that would help her prepare Mary to mother the Messiah (Luke 1:17)?

Q: Read Luke 2:16–19. How might Mary's "pondering" have included a recall of Elizabeth's exclamation in Luke 1:42? Explain your thoughts.

Q: We don't always have a complete understanding the first time we hear something. Even though Gabriel had told Mary and Joseph they were having God's Son, Jesus, what was their reaction to Simeon's prophecy (Luke 2:25–33)?

• Explain how Mary's time with Elizabeth might have prepared Mary to receive Simeon's "blessing" and unsettling words in Luke 2:34–35.

• How would you have reacted to Simeon's words?

Q: How do you now see spiritual mothering or mentoring as a "life investment?"

Q: Return to the question on page 74 where you rated yourself on passing down God's truths to the next generation. How have you become more effective in areas where you needed to improve?

Q: You have completed a study of generation-to-generation mentoring and the value of making a spiritual investment in another woman. Do you feel prepared to make that investment?

Q: Consider going through this study with another woman, or mentoring her in another area of her life. You now have knowledge that God wants invested in a spiritually younger woman. Make a commitment to God not to bury your talent.

M & M's

Q: Congratulations for the life investment you have made in each other by doing this study together! Like Elizabeth and Mary, you will see rewards for years to come. Now it's time to discuss how you each might make an investment in another woman's life.

Q: Mentor, encourage your mentee to become a mentor and do this study with another woman. While you probably will stay in each other's life, it's also time to look for another mentee.

Q: Mentee, you should be ready to mentor someone spiritually younger than yourself. You have grown and matured in this study, and you have that experience to share with another woman. Pray that God will give you the opportunity soon.

FACE-TO-FACE REFLECTIONS

God had an intentional purpose in sending Mary to Elizabeth, and Elizabeth rose to the occasion—in fact, she considered it an honor that God had chosen her to mentor Mary. Elizabeth had foresight that the lives of their two babies would intertwine, and that neither of the two boys would lead an easy life. Mary needed someone to prepare her for pregnancy and giving birth to the Messiah, but more importantly, she needed someone who understood and had insight into what His future would entail.

As mentors and spiritual mothers, we are not usually privy to the future of our mentees, but we do know one thing is sure—the Scriptures warn us that life will not always be easy. There will be times of great fortune and happiness and there will be down times of sadness and grief. We can be influencers in spiritually younger women's lives by assuring them that no matter what the circumstance, God will never leave them nor forsake them.

We don't always get the privilege of seeing the return on the investment that we make in someone else's life, but God sees it all. Many mentees will look back years later and realize the impact their mentor had in their life and thank God for the time they had together. And truly, isn't that why we mentor; not to build ourselves up or to get an earthly reward, but simply to know that we have been a part of helping someone grow closer to the Lord. They, in turn, will help someone else; and so we pay it forward in the kingdom of God.

PERSONAL PARABLE

As I watched mentors in the Woman to Woman Mentoring Ministry return to mentor again, I wanted to do something to commemorate their service. I came up with the idea of a Life Investment pin. We would add charms to the pin each time the mentor made a new life investment in a mentee. I got the idea from the mothers' and grandmothers' pins that have a charm for each child and grandchild. Since the mentors were spiritual mothers, I knew they would wear the pins with the same pride and honor.

But the true blessing comes when a mentor sees one of her former mentees wearing a Life Investment pin herself: that is tangible interest on her investment and deserves a "well done my good and faithful servant."

We had to add an extra chain to the original Life Investment pin because it only held five charms, and we have women who have invested their lives seven and eight times!

Elizabeth would have proudly worn a Life Investment pin, knowing that someday, Mary would wear one too.

Mentoring Moment

"Give me a generation of Christian mothers, [and spiritual mothers] and I will undertake to change the whole face of society in twelve months." — Lord Shaftesbury

FAITH IN ACTION

What one thing from this session does God want you to apply in your life today?

LET'S PRAY TOGETHER

Dear Father in heaven, we want to serve You unselfishly and learn to pour our lives into others. Help us use the wisdom and knowledge that You have bestowed upon us to enlighten and mature fellow believers. We must learn to take the focus off ourselves and love each other more than we love ourselves! We know that is impossible without You, but we also know that we can do all things through Christ who gives us strength. We love You, Lord. Help us learn to love others enough to invest in their spiritual future. Amen.

A GENERATION-TO-GENERATION TESTIMONY

ROSALIE CAMPBELL

Just like Mary, Sandra showed up on Rosalie's doorstep, and just like Elizabeth, Rosalie welcomed her into her home and her life. Sandra sought out a spiritual mother, a mentor, when life's circumstances called for godly wisdom, advice, and comfort.

While the Rose Bowl football game flashed across our TV screen on New Year's Day, I received a phone call from a young woman named Sarah that I knew from church. In a shaky, weak voice, she asked, "Would it be all right if I come over to talk to you?" Surprised at the call, I answered, "You mean today?" "Yes, today!" she replied.

Sensing the urgency in her tone, I agreed. Sandra arrived at my home with tears in her eyes. She cried as she blurted out, "My husband came home last week and told me he didn't want to be married to me anymore." I felt her anguish. I'd "been there and done that." I heard those very words from my own husband years before when he phoned to tell me he was moving out that day.

For two hours, this heartbroken young woman poured out the sad details: her husband came home one night before Christmas and told her he didn't think he loved her anymore. Sandra struggled to continue talking about her painful marital situation. I listened intently and tried to console her. She was confused, frightened, and full of questions as to why this was happening to her. Sandra timidly pleaded, "Would you have time to meet with me each week for awhile? I really need someone to help me through this."

Without hesitation, I agreed. Only a few weeks before her visit, I grabbed my new calendar, stared at the blank squares of each month, and pondered how I could spend my time more wisely in the coming year. After some prayer, I set a goal for the new millennium: to be a mentor. I wanted to reach out to someone and make a difference in her life as a compassionate woman had done for me years before. When I asked God to give me an opportunity to mentor someone, He didn't waste any time. I didn't have to go looking for someone because He had stirred Sandra's heart to seek me.

During our first visits together, Sandra and I talked mainly about her needs. When her husband pulled away from her, she fought loneliness and depression. She was at a loss for words when her four young children asked why she was crying all the time. A month after we started meeting, Sandra found out her husband was having an affair. Her self-esteem plummeted even deeper. During those first dark weeks, we focused on prayer with thanksgiving, believing God would heal her broken marriage. As she relied on God's promises, His words, faithfulness, and love uplifted Sandra.

We also set goals, kept a calendar of dates for our meetings and activities, and we decided to do a Bible study. Sandra wasn't the only one who benefited from this one-on-one relationship. When I struggled with difficult circumstances or situations in my own life, Sandra encouraged me. We both received many blessings from our fellowship and prayertimes.

Within two months, Sandra's prodigal husband finally came to his senses. He left the other woman when he realized he had a treasure at home—a godly wife who loved him patiently through the rough times. He repented, and sought a male Christian mentor who would guide him in God's ways. Today, Sandra's marriage has mended and is stronger than it ever was before.

FACE TO FACE WITH ELIZABETH AND MARY:
GENERATION *to* GENERATION

CLOSING
MATERIALS

THE JOURNEY ENDS

WE CONCLUDE OUR STUDY OF ELIZABETH AND MARY

LET'S PRAY A CLOSING PRAYER TOGETHER

Father, help us always to look for the way You are going to use the circumstances in our life to assist someone else. Let us not dwell on the difficult times, but delight in the way You use them to grow us and then use us to bless someone else who might be going through the same thing. Help us sincerely to rejoice when others succeed and not let jealousy and pride block the blessing we could receive from sharing in their joy. Let us look this very day for someone to bless or comfort with the love You pour down on them and us. Please help us be humble and open to the plans and purpose You have for our life. Keep us always searching for the spiritually older woman who could be our Elizabeth, and help us always to be aware of the Mary needing a spiritual mother. We love You, Lord. Amen.

JANET'S SUGGESTION:
Read Susan Hunt's book *Spiritual Mothering* for more on this facet of mentoring.

Use the Prayer & Praise Journal on pages 139–142. Record your spiritual journey and the things you have seen the Lord do in your life. For M&M'S, you will have a legacy of your mentoring relationship.

In *Praying for Your Prodigal Daughter: Hope, Help, & Encouragement for Hurting Parents* (Howard Books/Simon & Schuster, 2008), you can read about the miraculous story of praying home my former prodigal daughter, Kim. I also offer encouragement and tips to help parents of prodigals pray for their daughters.

My book *Dear God, They Say It's Cancer: A Companion Guide for Women on the Breast Cancer Journey* (Howard Books/Simon & Schuster, 2006), is my opportunity to mentor other breast-cancer sisters from my own journey.

Woman to Woman Mentoring How to Start, Grow, and Maintain a Mentoring Ministry DVD Leader Kit is available at your local LifeWay bookstore or at www.lifeway.com or by calling 1-800-458-2772.

Additional "Face-to-Face" Bible studies:
   Face-to-Face with Naomi and Ruth: Together for the Journey
   Face-to-Face with Mary and Martha: Sisters in Christ
   Face-to-Face with Euodia and Syntyche: From Conflict to Community

To learn more about AHW Ministries, Janet's writing and speaking ministry, visit www.womantowomanmentoring.com.

LEADER'S GUIDE

FOR GROUP-STUDY FACILITATORS AND M&M'S

SUGGESTIONS FOR FACILITATORS

Congratulations! God has appointed you the awesome privilege of setting the pace and focus for this group. Regardless of how many groups you have facilitated, this group will be a new and unique experience. This guide's suggestions and tips have helped me, and I trust they also will benefit you. Change or adapt them as you wish, but they are a solid place to start.

ORGANIZING THE SESSIONS

Small groups generally meet in a home, and larger churchwide groups usually meet at the church or other facility. I suggest for the larger group that you form small groups by sitting everyone at round tables. Appoint or ask for a volunteer facilitator for each table and have the group sit together for the five sessions of this study. Then both small-group leaders and large-group table facilitators can use the following format.

1. **Starting the sessions** — In my experience, members usually come in rushed, harried, and someone is always late — creating the perplexing dilemma of when to start. I suggest beginning on time because you are committed to ending on time. Don't wait for the last late person to arrive. Waiting dishonors those who arrive on time and sets the precedent that it's OK to be a little late because "they won't

start without me, anyway." Also, if you delay the start time, you may not finish the discussion.

2.   **Icebreakers**—Each session has an "icebreaker" that is fun, interactive, helps the group become acquainted, and encourages on-time arrivals. It's an interactive activity participants won't want to miss. The icebreaker also eases group members, to relax from their hectic day and move into a study mode.

3.   **Format**—Each session includes: Opening Prayer, Icebreaker, Five Days of Selected Discussion Questions, Prayer, Fellowship.

4.   **The Session Guide provides you with:**

- Preparation: what you need to do or obtain in advance.
- Icebreakers: openers for each meeting.
- **Bold type** indicates the action you need to say or take.
- Ideas: to help facilitate discussion and suggest answers that might be less obvious.
- Session name, day, and page number: to identify area discussed.

5.   **Suggested time**—Each session has nine numbered activities. Fifteen minutes on each number equals a two-hour meeting. This is a guideline to modify according to your time allotment. Let the Holy Spirit guide you and cover what seems applicable and pertinent to your group.

6.   **Facilitating discussion**—Questions and Scriptures to discuss are only a suggestion to enhance what participants have studied on their own already. Feel free to cover whatever material you think or the group feels is pertinent. Think about ways to:

- Keep all engaged in conversation.
- Avoid "rabbit trails."
- Assure each one has a clear understanding of the points under discussion.
- Encourage members to stay accountable by doing their lesson and arriving on time.

Big job you say! You can do it with God's help and strength.

7.   **Prayertime**—Prayer should be an ongoing and vital part of your group. Open and close your times together in prayer. There is a prayer at the end of each session, to pray together. Taking prayer requests can often get lengthy and be a source of gossip, if not handled properly. Let me share with you a way that works well in groups:

- At the end of the meeting, give each woman an index card and instruct her to write *one* prayer request pertaining to the study and pass the card to the leader/facilitator. Mix up the cards and have each person pick one. If someone picks her own card, have her put it back in the pile and pick a different one.
- When everyone has a card, go around the group (or table) and each person is to read the name and prayer request on her card so others can write down the requests. Participants may want to use the Prayer & Praise Journal starting on page 139.
- Instruct the group to hold hands and agree in unison as each participant prays the prayer request for the person whose card she has. This allows everyone to experience praying.
- Each woman takes home the card she received and prays for that person, ongoing.
- As the leader/facilitator, pray between meetings for the group, your leadership, and ask God to mentor you and the members. And have fun!

8. **Communion**—You will offer communion during the last session (assuming doing so creates no problems in your church context). Remind the group that taking communion together as believers is significant and unifying in three ways, by:
- proclaiming the Lord's death
- providing an opportunity for fellowship and unity
- giving participants an occasion for remembrance of Jesus

If there are nonbelievers, explain that communion is for believers. This is a perfect opportunity to ask if they would like to accept Jesus Christ as their Savior and pray the Salvation Prayer on page 82. If they are not ready, then ask them to sit quietly while the believers take communion. Ask someone to read aloud the Scriptures in Matthew 26:26–29 or Luke 22:14–20 and have the group partake of the juice and bread at the appropriate spot in the Scripture reading. Matthew 26:30 says, *"When they had sung a hymn they went out to the Mount of Olives."* Close the time of communion with a worship song.

9. **Fellowship time**—It's important for relationships to develop so group members feel comfortable sharing during discussions. A social time with refreshments provides a nice way to bring closure to the evening and allows time to chat. Encourage everyone to stay. Fellowship is part of the small group experience and allows larger groups to get to know other members.

M & M'S

Use the Session Guide for additional information and help in determining which questions to emphasize during meetings.

SESSION GUIDES

SESSION ONE—THEIR STORY

1. **Opening Prayer: Hold hands** as a group and **open** in prayer.

2. **Icebreaker: Can You Relate?**
Q: **Ask** if they could relate to Janet's opening story. There will probably be some shaking of heads in agreement and a few will exclaim, "Oh, Yes!"
Q: **Ask** group members to pair up with someone and each take 5 minutes briefly telling the other person about an "Elizabeth" or "spiritual mother" experience in her life.
Q: At the end of 10 minutes, **call** on a few members to describe the Elizabeth or spiritual mother experience in their discussion partner's life.

3. **Day One: How Does Elizabeth and Mary's Story Relate to Us?, Page 16**
Q: **Ask** each member of the group to read aloud a specified number of verses of Luke 1:5–80.
Q: **Ask** several to share what impressed them most about this story, or what seemed unusual.
Q: **Ask** if God revealed new insights to anyone.
♦ **Lead** a discussion of those who would like to share how their story is similar to Elizabeth and Mary's story.

4. **Day Two: What Is a Spiritual Mother?, Page 19**
Q: **Ask** several members to share their definition of *spiritual mother*.
♦ **Lead** a discussion on mentoring as spiritual mothering.
♦ **Lead** a discussion of Susan Hunt's quotes in the Mentoring Moment on page 20.

5. **Day Three: Characteristics of a Spiritual Mother, Page 21**
Q: **Ask** volunteers to give their definition of *righteous*.
Q: **Ask:** Why was being in Aaron's heritage significant? (They should arrive at: Aaron was Moses's brother, who along with his sons became a priest; Abijah was a priest in Aaron's lineage; and

Zechariah was in Abijah's priestly division. Elizabeth was also from the line of Aaron. So they both had rich spiritual heritage dating back to Moses.)

Q: **Lead** a discussion of the type of marriage they think Zechariah and Elizabeth had.

Q: **Discuss** the character qualities they discovered in Elizabeth.

Q: **Ask** two people to read Proverbs 31:25–30 and Hebrews 13:7, and **discuss** how these verses offer guidelines for finding a mentor/spiritual mother.

Q: **Ask:** Why did Elizabeth make a good spiritual mother to Mary?

6. **Day Four: Finding a Spiritual Mother, Page 24**

Q: **Ask** what *"In the sixth month"* refers to in Luke 1:26. **Point out** that it is referring to the previous verses in Luke 1:24–25.

♦ **Discuss** the prophetic reasons Scripture gives for Elizabeth being pregnant before Mary.

Q: **Ask** each woman to describe in one sentence a current good and difficult circumstance that she would like to talk about to someone who has experienced something similar.

♦ **Ask** if the group could see how God could use those same circumstances in their life to help someone else who might be going through a similar situation.

Q: **Discuss** where to find a spiritual mother and where to find someone who needs a spiritual mother.

Q: **Ask:** What does Matthew 21:22 and Mark 11:24 instruct you to do before seeking a spiritual mother or mentor? (Answer: pray)

7. **Day Five: Women of Faith, Page 27**

Q: **Assign** someone to be Abraham, Sarah, Zechariah, Joseph, Elizabeth, Mary, and Simeon.

♦ **Instruct** each person to say how God spoke to him or her and then recite, in character, his or her response (read from appropriate Scripture passage).

♦ **Encourage** them to speak in the first-person using the tone of voice, mannerisms, and language the biblical character would use.

Q: **Lead** a "spirited" discussion of how God "intervened" in biblical days and how He still intervenes in our lives today.

Q: **Ask** what excuses Mary might have given Gabriel for not being ready to yield completely to God's plan.

Q: **Ask** how the verses in Psalms will equip them to see God more clearly in the everyday.

Q: **Encourage** those who haven't yet become aware of the supernatural power of God in their life to be comforted by John 20:29, Romans 8:24–25, and Hebrews 11:1. **Commend** them for faithfully believing in what they haven't seen yet and for patiently remaining hopeful until they do.

♦ **Remind them** that becoming a Christian is evidence of the hand of God in their life.

Q: **Ask** several to share the paragraph they wrote about Elizabeth's and Mary's faith, modeled after Hebrews 11.

Q: **Ask** volunteers to share a time when others didn't believe their story of a God-incident.

Q: **Ask:** How many got the right answer to finding the "f" riddle?

♦ **Ask:** How did this exercise open your eyes to other things you might be overlooking, like God's presence in your life?

Q: **Ask** each woman to share the one thing that ministered to her the most in this session and any action goals she has set for herself.

Q: **Instruct** everyone to bring a picture to the next meeting of a woman who has been her "Elizabeth" or mentor. This could be a family member or friend. **Advise** them to write this assignment down so they won't forget.

8. Prayertime (See Leader's Guide Page 121)
Prayer request, prayer partner exchange, and group prayer

9. Fellowship and Refreshments

SESSION TWO–WE ARE FAMILY

● **Call** during the week to remind everyone to bring a picture of her "Elizabeth" or mentor.

1. Opening Prayer: Hold hands as a group and **open** in prayer.

2. Icebreaker:

Q: **Ask** each person to show the picture she brought of a woman who has been an Elizabeth, mentor, or significant influence in her life.

Q: **Give** each woman about three minutes to explain the relationship.

3. **Day One: How Will Spiritual Mothering Affect My Family?, Page 34**

Q: **Ask** for reasons they believe Mary went such a long distance to see Elizabeth instead of staying home with her mom or asking Elizabeth to come to her.

Q: **Ask:** How do you think Mary's mother might have reacted to the trip?

Q: **Ask** someone to share how their own mother would react to them seeking out a spiritual mother.

Q: **Discuss** how they would act if their daughter sought out a spiritual mother.

4. **Day Two: Mentoring Our Family, Page 37**

Q: **Read** and **discuss** 1 Timothy 5:8.

Q: **Ask** someone to share an experience similar to Mary's going to an extended family member for godly advice or counseling.

◆ **Ask** if they thought about how this might have affected or had an impact on that family member?

Q: **Ask** if anyone has ever been the person to give godly advice or council to a family member?

◆ For those who haven't had this experience, **ask** if they have considered what they might do to make themselves available to other family members?

5. **Day Three: The Family of God, Page 40**

Q: **Break** into four groups and **assign** two Scriptures on page 40 to each group.

◆ **Give** them 10 minutes to discuss what the verses say about Christians being family and how we are to treat each other.

◆ **Instruct** them to pick a spokesperson to report back their findings to the whole group.

Q: **Reconvene** as a group and **call on** each spokesperson to share the consensus of the group.

Q: **Ask** if the rest of the group has any questions or comments after each report.

Q: **Lead** a discussion on ways they balance their personal family and extended Christian family.

6. **Day Four: Making Time for "Family," Page 43**

Q: **Ask:** If you were Mary, do you think you would have made the trip to see Elizabeth?

Q: **Lead** a discussion of what they noticed about Elizabeth's response to Mary's unannounced visit.

Q: **Discuss** the compromises and sacrifices that everyone makes in order to have time for a new relationship.

Q: **Ask:** Why do you think we let things get in the way of time with others?

Q: **Ask** for suggestions of ways they are willing to change their own schedules to make more time for relationships.

Q: **Ask** for ideas of things they could do together with another woman in the group. **Stress** that God makes time in our lives for things He thinks are important.

♦ **Point out** the benefits of looking through God's eyes at our busy schedules. **Remind** them that when you give your time and schedule to the Lord, you have more energy to get the things done that He wants you to accomplish.

7. **Day Five: A Husband of Noble Character, Who Can Find?, Page 47**

Q: **Discuss** what they learned about Zechariah from Luke 1:5–8.

Q: **Ask:** What had Zechariah prayed for?

Q: **Read** together Luke 1:67–79. **Discuss** the insight and prophecy that Zechariah includes in this song.

♦ **Ask:** What can you discern about Zechariah from this song?

Q: **Lead** a discussion of how Joseph displays virtue and honor in his dealing with Mary's pregnancy.

Q: **Be sensitive** to any unmarried women in your group, but also stress that Zechariah and Joseph are the kind of men you want for a husband; until then, let God be your husband.

8. **Prayertime**

♦ Prayer request, prayer partner exchange, and group prayer.

9. **Fellowship and Refreshments**

SESSION THREE—WE ARE DIFFERENT

● **Have** index cards for everyone in your group.

● **Write** on each card a different age ranging from 20 to 90.

● **Have** a white board and marker.

1. **Opening Prayer: Hold hands** as a group and **open** in prayer.

2. **Icebreaker:**
Q: **Turn** the prepared index cards upside down and have each member pick a card.
Q: **Ask:** What would a woman of the age on your card probably think about girls wearing shorts to school?
Q: **Give** them a moment to think about their answer.
Q: **Have** fun discussing how the answers relate to age.

3. **Day One: Things in Common, and Not So Common, Page 52**
Q: **Discuss** the things Elizabeth and Mary had in common. Here are a few obvious and not so obvious commonalities:
   - pregnant under unusual circumstances that most people wouldn't understand
   - recipient of God's grace: Elizabeth beat the biological clock and Mary chosen to carry the Messiah
   - babies had an intricately related historical mission
   - strong belief in the Lord
   - husbands told by Gabriel what to name their babies, which was not the traditional naming of the first-born son after his earthly father
   - humility
   - not jealous or competitive
   - sons had special assignment from God
   - Elizabeth's son would be the forerunner of Mary's son's ministry
   - sons would be misunderstood and die a violent death
   - visitation by Gabriel
Q: **Ask** what some of Elizabeth's and Mary's differences were? **Be sure** they include:
   - big age difference
   - from different generations
   - from two different social structures. Elizabeth's husband was a priest so they held a respected prominent position in the community. Mary was marrying a carpenter.
   - Elizabeth lived in the hill country, which means that Mary must have lived in the flat lands.
   - Elizabeth had a home and was a homemaker. Mary had not even left her parents' home yet.

- Elizabeth went into seclusion for the first five months of her pregnancy, and Mary publicly took a trip in her first, third, and ninth month of pregnancy.
- Elderly Elizabeth may have moved slowly and lacked energy. Mary had the energy and movements of a teenager.

Q: **Ask:** How does 1 Corinthians 12:4–6 instruct us to treat those who are different than us?

♦ **Point out** that we don't always initially see why God put us together in a spiritual or mentoring relationship. But we often look back later and see that He was at work in the similarities and differences in our relationships.

Q: **Ask:** Has anyone ever sought out a relationship with a significantly older or younger woman? Explain.

4. **Day Two: Husband and Wife Differences, Page 56**

Q: **Have fun** discussing some of the "marriage" questions Mary might have asked Elizabeth and why it would be easier to ask Elizabeth instead of Mary's mom.

Q: **Make** two columns on the white board and head one side "Differences," and the other side "Why God Made Us Different."

♦ **Ask:** What are some universal differences between men and women? As they shout out differences, **have someone write** them under the "Differences" column.

♦ When they have exhausted the differences, **go back and ask** them to give the reason they think God created each difference and write their answer in the opposite column.

Q: **Divide** the group in half and **assign** one group to discuss the Scriptures on page 57 that help wives support their husbands, and the other group to discuss the Scriptures that show husbands how to support their wives.

Q: **Regroup** and **ask** for a summary of the discussion in each group.

5. **Day Three: When You're Spiritually Older than Your Husband, Page 60**

Q: **Ask** for their answers to why it was significant that Zechariah and Elizabeth lived in the time of a wicked king's rule? One answer: it would have been very difficult to remain pious and maintain the godly life of this couple.

closing materials

Q: **Ask:** Why was Joseph's heritage important? (Answer: Prophecy said the Messiah would come from the line of David, and Joseph was a descendent of David.)

Q: **Lead** a discussion of the complete faith that Elizabeth and Mary displayed in contrast with Zechariah's and Joseph's initial doubt.

Q: **Ask:** Why do you think God removed Zechariah's voice?

◆ **Ask:** Why did he get his voice back? (Answer: He believed).

Q: **Ask** if anyone wants to share a time when God silenced her.

Q: **Ask:** How do you think Elizabeth handled Zechariah's discipline?

◆ How could this experience help Elizabeth mentor Mary in dealing with Joseph's first reaction to divorce her?

Q: **Ask:** What instruction does 1 Peter 3:1–2, 15–16 give to wives who are more spiritually mature than their husbands?

If there are any group members with unbelieving husbands or husbands that are newer in the faith than the wife is, **ask** them to share how this session encouraged them.

Q: **Have someone read** 1 Corinthians 11:1, 11 and discuss what it means for the husband to be the head of the home.

6. **Day Four: One Is Chosen, One Is Not, Page 65**

Q: **Discuss** what Elizabeth had in common with Sarah, Rachel, and Hannah.

Q: **Have someone read** Genesis 30:1 and Romans 12:10.

◆ **Lead** a discussion of their thoughts on Elizabeth's reaction to Mary being chosen instead of her for the blessing of mothering the Messiah.

◆ **Make** sure they note that Mary didn't brag about carrying the Messiah, and Elizabeth wasn't jealous that God chose Mary to carry the Messiah when Elizabeth was older, wiser, and had waited longer for a child.

Q: **Ask:** How would you have responded?

Q: **Ask** if anyone would like to give a testimony of being truly happy for someone selected instead of them for an honor.

Q: **Ask** someone else to share a time when they were the one selected for an honor.

◆ Were they sensitive to those who weren't selected?

◆ If not, what have they learned from Mary?

Q: **Discuss** Jill Briscoe's quote in the Mentoring Moment.

♦ **Ask:** Who likes to play second fiddle to someone else? **Be sure** they note that while second fiddle may not be prestigious, it is just as valuable to the orchestra as the first fiddle.

7. **Day Five: What Will Others Think?, Page 68**

Q: **Ask** for the reasons they thought Elizabeth stayed in seclusion.

Q: **Discuss** how Elizabeth could have mentored Mary in how to withstand stares and hurtful comments.

Q: **Ask:** How important is it to you what other people think of you?

Q: **Discuss** the Personal Parable on page 70 and how each of them reacted to the news of former Governor Sarah Palin's unwed pregnant daughter? How did the media react?

Q: **Ask** volunteers to pretend they are a newscaster reporting the news of:

1. Priest Zechariah's loss of voice.
2. Elizabeth's pregnancy.
3. Mary's pregnancy.

Q: **Ask:** What should be our reaction to these events as Christians?

Q: **Discuss** a community project for the group to do together to help disadvantaged women.

8. **Prayertime**

Prayer request, prayer partner exchange, and group prayer.

9. **Fellowship and Refreshments**

SESSION FOUR–MOTHER KNOWS BEST

● **Have** a white board and markers.
● **Have** index cards.
● **Think** of several examples of cliché sayings mothers and grandmothers often say, such as, "If it's not one thing, it's another." Or "We'll just have to see about that." Or "Put on your coat. You'll be chilled to the bone." Or think of some of your own.

1. **Opening Prayer: Hold hands** as a group and **open** in prayer.

2 **Icebreaker:**

Q: **Pass out** an index card to each woman.

Q: **Instruct** them to write three cliché sayings their grandmother or mother always say. **Provide** examples to get them going. **Tell** them not to put their names on the cards.

Q: **Have them** turn the cards back into you. **Shuffle** the cards and have everyone **pick a card**, making sure they don't get their own card back.

Q: **Have each** woman **read aloud** the sayings on the card she received and then **guess** whose card it is. When the owner of the card identifies herself, she can give any extra explanation or history of the sayings.

3. Day One: From Generation to Generation, Page 73

Q: **Discuss** the meaning of Mary's words in Luke 1:48–50.

Q: **Have** volunteers read the Scriptures on pages 73-74. Then **lead** a discussion of the obligations one generation has to the next.

Q: **Ask** how they saw Elizabeth and Mary's relationship fulfilling these Scriptures.

Q: **Ask** volunteers to share how they rated themselves in fulfilling these Scriptures.

4. Day Two: A Two-Way Relationship, Page 77

Q: **Ask** someone to read Romans 5:3–5 and **discuss** how Elizabeth role modeled these verses to Mary.

♦ **Ask:** What were some of Elizabeth's character building experiences?

♦ **Discuss** how Elizabeth could use these experiences to help Mary. **Be sure** they include: infertility, disgrace, disbelief by others, feeling like a freak of nature, dealing with her husband's reaction, center of gossip and stares.

♦ **Reinforce** that mentoring is always a two-way relationship and never a hierarchy.

♦ **Point out** that mentors benefit from the prayers and support of the mentee.

Q: **Point out** that as God helps us through circumstances in life, He may put someone in our path who is going through something similar so we can share with them the comfort and peace of having the Lord in our life.

Q: **Ask:** What are some practical things Elizabeth could have taught Mary?

Q: **Ask:** How could Mary help Elizabeth?

Q: **Ask** them to share ways they have experienced the "two-way" concept in relationships, or specifically, if anyone has experienced this in a mentoring relationship.

5. **Day Three: Filled with the Spirit, Page 80**

Q: **Make sure** they know that the answer to the first two questions is that they were all filled with the Holy Spirit.

Q: **Assign the reading aloud** of the Scriptures regarding *"filled with the Spirit"* on page 80. **Facilitate** a discussion on being *"filled with the Spirit."*

Q: **Ask:** How do we become filled with the Spirit? (The answer: The first step is accepting Jesus Christ as our Savior and becoming a believer. After which, answers might be: by asking, praying, confessing sins, reading God's Word, etc.)

Q: **Ask:** How does being filled with the Spirit help us lead godly lives?

Q: **Ask:** How do you see Elizabeth displaying the fruit of the Spirit in her reception of Mary?

Q: **Ask** if anyone made a commitment for Christ or rededicated her life during this session, or if anyone wants to do it right now. If it is the latter, have everyone bow their heads and lead that person through the Salvation Prayer on page 82.

◆ **Celebrate** and **congratulate** any new believers.

6. **Day Four: An Encouraging Word, Page 84**

Q: **Ask** each woman to read a Scripture on page 84 and share how she saw Elizabeth and Mary living out the passage.

Q: **Ask** someone to read James 3:5–12 and **lead** a discussion on the power of the tongue.

◆ **Ask:** Who can tame our tongue? (Answer: God)

Q: **Ask** for several testimonies of someone encouraging them in a difficult situation.

Q: **Encourage** someone else to give a testimony of being the encourager.

Q: **Ask** the group to come up with ways they could offer encouragement to each other, and **ask** someone to write their suggestions on the white board.

Q: **Ask** each woman to commit to doing one thing on the list for another member in the group before they meet again.

closing materials

7. **Day Five: Judgment or Discernment?, Page 87**

Q: **Ask:** What is the common theme of the people who understood and accepted that God was working through Elizabeth, Zechariah, Mary, and Joseph? (Answer: they prayed and worshipped).

Q: **Discuss** what Matthew 7:1–5 tells us to do before we criticize or judge.

◆ **Ask:** How many actually do this?

Q: **Ask** several to share their paraphrase of Proverbs 10:19–21.

◆ **Have someone read** Romans 12:2–3. **Ask:** What does it mean to have a renewed mind?

Q: **Ask** how they determine if they are judging or discerning?

Q: **Ask** them to share their thoughts on how to be a discerning person. **Be sure** they include:

● prayer
● studying the Bible
● reading books by Christian authors
● consulting Christian counsel

Q: **Ask:** How would looking for the best in people help in exercising discernment?

Q: **Ask:** How do you view the younger and older generation? Are you critical? Judgmental? Understanding? Tolerant?

◆ **Discuss** ways to improve relationships with the next generation — older or younger.

Q: **Facilitate** discussion of the answers they gave for how they would have received Elizabeth's story and Mary's story. Response? Thoughts? Words? Actions?

Q: **Lead** a discussion of how the two questions in the Face-to-Face Reflections — "What is my motivation?" and "Is my perspective in agreement with God's perspective?" — would help in determining if you're being judgmental or discerning.

Q: **Talk** about ways to establish an accountability mentoring relationship (see Face-to-Face Reflections page 90–91). **Point out** that if the mentee wants accountability, she needs to give the mentor permission to ask her about the area of concern. Next, they need to agree on encouraging ways to accomplish this.

◆ **Break** the group into pairs.

◆ **Assign** one member of the pair to be the accountability partner (mentor) and the other to be the person needing accountability (mentee).

♦ **Randomly give** each pair an area of accountability i.e., eating, finances, watching TV, or playing computer games.

♦ **Give** them about 10 minutes to role-play:
1. Asking for accountability
2. Giving permission to be held accountable
3. Establishing encouraging ways to be held accountable

♦ **Bring** the group back together and **discuss** how successful they think they were at this exercise and how it felt to go through the process.

8. **Prayertime**
Prayer request, prayer partner exchange, and group prayer.

9. **Fellowship and Refreshments**

SESSION FIVE–WORSHIPPING TOGETHER

● **Prayerfully pick out** several worship songs on CDs that convey the theme of this study.

● **Have** the words available for everyone to sing along.

● **Bring** a CD player or check to see if the hostess has one.

1. **Opening Prayer: Hold hands** as a group and **open** in prayer.

2. **Icebreaker:**
Q: **Ask** for sharing of how they encouraged each other since last session.

Q: **Lead** them through a worship time of singing and praising the Lord.

3. **Day One: A Spiritual Relationship, Page 94**
Q: **Lead** a discussion of the spiritual attributes they saw in Elizabeth and how she might have used them to disciple Mary.

Q: **Ask** each person to identify one of Elizabeth's spiritual attributes that she excels in and one she needs to work on.

Q: **Discuss** the spiritual maturity in Mary between Luke 1:28–29 and Luke 1:46–55.

Q: **Ask** two volunteers to **act out** how Mary and Elizabeth would greet each other if both had been trying to tell their story of what happened to them and how they were being treated.

- Next **have** two other volunteers **act out** how they actually greeted each other in Luke 1:40–55.
- **Discuss** the differences in the two greetings.

Q: Ask someone to read Psalm 100:2. **Discuss** how Elizabeth and Mary worshiped according to this Psalm.

Q: **Read** Romans 12:1 and **lead** a discussion of sacrifice as a form of worship.

- **Ask:** How Elizabeth and Mary epitomized this verse.

Q: **Ask:** How did A. W. Tozer's quote in the Mentoring Moment on page 97 give you a new appreciation of worship?

4. Day Two: Nothing Is Impossible with God, Page 98

Q: **Ask:** How did Gabriel explain the "impossible" in Mary's and Elizabeth's life?

Q: **Lead** a discussion of how each Scripture on page 98 explains the seemingly "impossible circumstances" that happen in a believer's life.

Q: **Read aloud** Hebrews 11:6 and **be sure** they admit how hard it is to believe God can do the impossible.

Q: **Lead** a discussion of the observers' reaction to Zechariah exiting the temple voiceless and then getting his voice back, and Elizabeth having a baby.

Q: **Ask:** Why does God publicly perform the "impossible?"

- **Be sure** they conclude that the onlookers knew that God was at the center of these "impossible circumstances," and that is one of the reasons God does miracles publicly—so God gets the glory and others will be drawn to Him.

Q: **Ask:** What helps you trust in God in the midst of impossible circumstances?

Q: **Ask** volunteers to share a time in their life where God did the impossible and how it affected those who observed the miracle.

Q: **Discuss** this statement in the Face-to-Face Reflection on page 100: no human being can do the impossible no matter how much he or she thinks it is by his or her power, it is not.

5. Day Three: Listening to God, Page 102

Q: **Lead** a discussion of what they learned about listening from the verses on page 102.

Q: **Ask:** Who is God's voice to believers today? They should respond: the Holy Spirit.

Q: **Ask:** Who can actually identify the Holy Spirit prompting you?

♦ **Ask** several to give examples of responding to the promptings.

♦ **Ask** for others to share when they have felt prompted but haven't responded. For example, knew you should give someone a phone call, but didn't.

♦ If anyone is unsure about the Holy Spirit and God's work in a believer's life, **discuss** the significance of Luke 3:16, and John 14:15–19, 26.

Q: **Read** Psalm 119:11 and John 1:1. **Ask:** What other ways does God speak to us?

Q: **Determine** who is having a regular quiet time, and **ask** the others if they would like the group to keep them accountable.

6. Day Four: Our Prayers Are Heard, Praise God!, Page 106

Q: **Ask** how they saw Zechariah and Elizabeth patiently waiting on God for an answer to prayer and how surprised they must have been when He answered so many years later.

Q: **Discuss** what 1 Chronicles 5:20 and Hebrews 6:10–12 instruct us about answered prayer. **Point out** that God is to be glorified and praised.

Q: **Ask:** How did Zechariah know that their son John would be the forerunner of Jesus?

Q: **Lead** a discussion of why God had Zechariah and Elizabeth wait so long for a child.

(They should arrive at the conclusion that their child was going to be the forerunner of Jesus, so they had to wait for Mary to be old enough to have a child.)

Q: **Ask** for answers as to how Mary's visit confirmed God's plan for Elizabeth and Zechariah's baby.

Q: **Ask** several to share their comparison of Elizabeth's praise with Mary's praise song.

Q: **Ask:** How did you rate yourself at waiting for answered prayer?

Q: **Ask:** What is the antidote to anxiety? (Answer: prayer)

7. Day Five: Life Investment, Page 110

Q: **Have someone read** Matthew 25:14–30 and **discuss** how this parable applies to mentoring and Elizabeth's life investment in Mary.

♦ **Ask:** How did this investment prepare Mary for the future joys and heartaches of being the mother of Jesus?

Q: **Ask** how they see spiritual mothering or mentoring as a "life investment."

Q: **Ask:** What other ways can we invest our lives in others?

Q: **Ask:** Did anyone go back to page 74 and improve your scoring in passing down truths to the next generation?

Q: **Ask** others to share how they plan to make an investment in the next generation of believers.

Q: **Lead** a discussion of Rosalie Campbell's testimony. If needed, you can get the discussion going by asking questions like:
  ● What were your thoughts as you read it?
  ● How did knowing this was true impact you?
  ● What were similarities between Rosalie and Sandra's story and Elizabeth and Mary's story?

Wrap Up Time

Q: **Lead a discussion of:**
  ● How has this study influenced your understanding of the term *spiritual mother*?
  ● What in the study had the greatest impact on you?
  ● What will you be able to apply to your life?
  ● What equipped you to be a mentor/spiritual mother or seek out a mentor/spiritual mother?

Q: **Ask** for any other input they might have as you close this study.

8. Prayertime

Prayer request, prayer partner exchange, and group prayer.

♦ **Read** the closing prayer on page 118 together in unison.

♦ **Sing** a worship song and **read** one or two of the personalized Mary's Magnificat (page 107), as a closing to the worship time.

♦ **Take** Communion (see page 122).

9. Fellowship and Refreshments

Q: **Discuss** the next Bible Study they would like to do.

Q: **Look** on pages 119 and 144 for additional "Face-to-Face" Bible studies.

PRAYER & PRAISE JOURNAL

PRAYER & PRAISE JOURNAL

PRAYER & PRAISE JOURNAL

Prayer & Praise Journal